Teaching History in the Digital Age

DIGITAL HUMANITIES

The Digital Humanities series provides a forum for ground-breaking and benchmark work in digital humanities, lying at the intersections of computers and the disciplines of arts and humanities, library and information science, media and communications studies, and cultural studies.

Series Editors:

Julie Thompson Klein, Wayne State University
Tara McPherson, University of Southern California
Paul Conway, University of Michigan

———————

Manifesto for the Humanities: Transforming Doctoral Education in Good Enough Times
Sidonie Smith

Teaching History in the Digital Age
T. Mills Kelly

Hacking the Academy: New Approaches to Scholarship and Teaching from Digital Humanities
Daniel J. Cohen and Tom Scheinfeldt, Editors

Writing History in the Digital Age
Jack Dougherty and Kristen Nawrotzki, Editors

Pastplay: Teaching and Learning History with Technology
Kevin Kee, Editor

Interdisciplining Digital Humanities: Boundary Work in an Emerging Field
Julie Thompson Klein

Digital Rhetoric: Theory, Method, Practice
Douglas Eyman

Ethical Programs: Hospitality and the Rhetorics of Software
James J. Brown Jr.

———————

DIGITALCULTUREBOOKS, an imprint of the University of Michigan Press, is dedicated to publishing work in new media studies and the emerging field of digital humanities.

Teaching History

in the

Digital Age

< T. Mills Kelly >

The University of Michigan Press
Ann Arbor

First paperback edition 2016
Copyright © by T. Mills Kelly 2013
Some rights reserved

Published in the United States of America by
The University of Michigan Press
Manufactured in the United States of America
♾ Printed on acid-free paper

2019   2018   2017   2016   5   4   3   2

A CIP catalog record for this book is available from the British Library.

http://dx.doi.org/10.3998/dh.12146032.0001.001

Library of Congress Cataloging-in-Publication Data
    Kelly, T. Mills.
       Teaching history in the digital age / T. Mills Kelly.
          pages cm. — (Digital humanities)
       Includes bibliographical references.
       ISBN 978-0-472-11878-6 (hardback) — ISBN 978-0-472-02913-6 (e-book)
       1. History—Computer-assisted instruction.   2. History—Study and teaching
    (Higher)—Technological innovations.   I. Title.
       D16.255.C65K45   2013
       907.8'5—dc23

                                                                2012047396

ISBN 978-0-472-03676-9 (paper)

Preface

Historians are always a little nervous about the whole concept of "beginnings," because we know just how difficult it is to pin down, exactly, when something began. In the case of this book, though, it is not difficult for me to say exactly when it began. During the 1996–1997 academic year I was a visiting instructor in the Department of History at the University of New Hampshire. About a month into the fall semester, we all received a memo (not an email) from the campus IT staff asking "Do you want to learn how to put your syllabus on the World Wide Web?" I wish I had saved that memo, because it launched me down the path that led to this book.

I signed up for that workshop and over the course of two hours or so, learned enough basic HTML code to put my syllabus on the university's servers. That was in the days before even Netscape Composer, much less Dreamweaver, or any other website-building software, so we had to write our own code. I promptly put my syllabus up online and in class the next day told all my students they could now access their class syllabus on the Web (as we called it in those days). Because only about half of them had email addresses, I had to tell them in person. My naïve belief was that with the syllabus online 24/7, never again would a student be able to say to me, "Oh, Dr. Kelly, I didn't do the reading for today, because I couldn't find my syllabus." The online syllabus did eliminate that excuse, but, of course, they found others that were equally compelling—at least in their eyes. But that does not mean they did not work hard and try to learn what I was teaching them; it is just that technology did not change every dynamic of the college classroom—an important lesson we would do well to remember. That online syllabus did have a surprising result. When I got my end-of-semester survey results back, student after student wrote in their comments that the online syllabus was one of the best parts of the course—not my carefully crafted lectures, or those group learning exercises I spent so much time planning. On the one hand, I was disappointed that all the work I had done to create an exciting learning experience seemed to have had little impact. On the other, I was glad to have found something that sparked their interest.

Between the fall and spring semester that year I received a call from the director of the University of New Hampshire-Manchester campus who wanted to know if I could fill in at the last minute for one of their history faculty members who, for medical reasons, could not teach the first half of Western Civilization in the spring semester. I needed the money (our first child had been born just a few weeks earlier) and so I agreed, even though I had never taken a class in European history prior to 1600. When I informed the person offering me the job of this, he said something along the lines of, "That's okay, you'll know more about it than they do." Now that I direct a program at my university I know that sometimes we have to make such last-minute compromises to avoid canceling classes, but at the time, I was both thankful for the work and a little uncomfortable with the ethics of teaching a subject I was weak on. With a fair amount of trepidation, I designed a course, largely around the textbook, but included my first Internet-based assignment. I introduced my students to this new thing called the Internet (maybe I said World Wide Web), and explained that one could find many historical primary sources online using the Lynx web browser the university made available to us. These were all text-only sources—white text on a black screen. I wanted them to each find a source every week, print it out, bring it in, and we would talk about it. In this way, my students built a miniature library of primary sources for the class and I was saved from having to look up lots of sources on my own to supplement those in the document reader I had assigned. To my surprise and pleasure, our discussions of the sources my students found, as opposed to the ones I assigned, were the most interesting and generative conversations of the semester. That lesson—that students can take a very important role in their own learning—is another we would be wise to remember. Once again, at the end of the semester I heard from my students that the Internet assignment was the best part of the course. I was smart enough to realize I was onto something.

The following year, I was a sabbatical replacement instructor at Grinnell

College. While there, I built my first website and began to post resources online. I also designed several additional assignments that made use of resources others had posted online. In my second semester I even had my students build a website of their own—a small archive of primary sources. It was an assignment they enjoyed, but also found frustrating due to their low technical skills and the relatively high bar for entry into the world of creating online content in 1998. At some point in the spring semester, my department chair (the great Russian historian Dan Kaiser) asked me a very important question. Given the amount of time all that Internet stuff was taking—he did not say it was taking time from my traditional scholarship, but we both knew it was—how did I know that my students were learning better, or at least differently by working with online historical resources? I had no earthly idea. I knew they were enjoying what they were doing with the technology, and I think we can all agree that if students are engaged, something positive is probably happening. But I really did not know if they were learning better or worse.

My concern about whether or not all the time I was spending designing online learning experiences for my students was resulting in positive learning gains launched me into my first research in what we now call the scholarship of teaching and learning. That first project, eventually supported by a fellowship from the Carnegie Foundation for the Advancement of Teaching, resulted in an article in which I argued that there were, indeed, some measurable differences in how students learned when they had access to historical sources online.[1] I also learned from that project that very often—if not most often—the gains we see when students are using technology to learn about the past are typically pretty subtle, which is another way of saying that the grand pronouncements of the techno enthusiasts (I was one once) are rarely borne out when we look carefully at what students are actually doing.

I also learned the value of watching very carefully when my students use technology, both to make sense of the past and in their everyday lives. When you watch them carefully in this way, you see that they use the technology in ways that are both surprising and mundane. For every student who creates something brand-new that we had not anticipated, there are four or five who are just trying to get through the course and so use the technology to conjure up a few reasonable answers for today's discussion or next Friday's test. We know that our students are much closer to the cutting edges of the digital revolution than we are, but nothing I have seen in the past dozen years of close observation has altered my conviction that just because they are adept *users of* the technology, that is not the same thing as being adept *learners with* the technology. For history teachers, this is a very positive insight, because it means that we still have a lot to teach our students about the past and how to make sense of it, using both the analog tools we grew up with and the digital ones that pervade our students' lives. This book is my attempt to offer some guidance on how history teachers can do just that.

Because all of my teaching experience is at the post-secondary level, this book is aimed at those who teach history courses at the college level. However, over the past six years I have spent a great deal of time working with K–12 history teachers through various professional development workshops and in those interactions have learned that what we do starting in Grade 13 is not really that different from what happens beginning around the fourth grade. The sophistication of the problems posed and the sources assigned are greater, but the issues we grapple with when it comes to helping our students learn about the past are not that different. In those workshops, one of the exercises I put history teachers through is compiling a list of what historical thinking is and how we know it when we see it. The lists that primary- and secondary-school teachers come up with are not markedly different from the ones college faculty produce. For this reason, I hope that the questions raised in this book will be useful to anyone who teaches history, but especially those teaching Advanced Placement/International Baccalaureate courses in high schools and those teaching history at the college level.

No book that takes on the subject of how technological innovation is changing the landscape of a discipline can ever hope to keep up with the rapid pace of that innovation. The author must always decide that, at some point, new innovations cannot make their way into the current edition of the book, otherwise that book will never be finished. In my case, the up-and-coming innovation that I have had to set aside so that I could finish this book is mobile computing. Already in 2012 mobile computing has made some interesting inroads into the teaching and learning of history, but remains enough in its infancy that I will save a fuller examination of this topic for a possible second edition of this book. For now, I will say that I believe that mobile computing holds tremendous promise for helping our students learn about the past, in particular because it offers the possibility of putting students in the places where the history they are learning about actually happened.[2] While they cannot visit those places as they were long ago (or even relatively recently ago), it strikes me that there is something to be gained by forcing oneself to stand where the actors in a particular historical drama stood, to look out over vistas they looked over, even if those vistas are radically changed, and to contemplate how and why those changes had taken place. My first thinking about this issue began in January 2007 when I was standing in line outside the Jewish ghetto of Prague with a group of students from my university. Because I know the history of that neighborhood well, as I stood there shivering under a light snowfall, I looked up at the apartment building next door and wondered about the Jewish families who had lived there until they were deported to the concentration camp at Terezín. What, I wondered, would it be like to be able to pull out a smartphone and access information about those families? What if I could read their histories and possibly add my own reflections on those histories as part of some social web of information? From a technological standpoint, a mobile computing application such as the one I dreamed of that day is not difficult at all and versions of this idea have already appeared in the mobile marketplace. For now, in early 2012, they remain out of the repertoire of the history teacher and so I have not considered them in this book in any detail.

Finally, I hope to challenge the reader to consider just how different will be the world our students will live in once they leave our schools and colleges. History will still be history, but already the digital revolution sweeping through our culture (and cultures all across the globe) is transforming the ways that history is being made by historians, teachers, students, and enthusiasts. Historical writing is still historical writing, and will likely not look very different a decade from now. But writing, the way I am writing this book, is now only one way that history is being made, especially by those who have never known (or at least cannot remember) a world without the Internet, without wireless access, and without Google. The rising generation is making the technology their own, and so we should not be surprised that they are also beginning to use that technology to make history their own. Throughout this book I argue that historians need to get over the fact that the landscape of historical production has already shifted under our feet, and that it is time for us to accommodate our teaching to that shift. If we do not, our students will make history without us.

Acknowledgments

This book is dedicated to the memory of my colleague and friend Roy Rosenzweig, founder of the Center for History and New Media (CHNM) and one of the great historians of the twentieth century.[1] Had it not been for Roy, I would not have been hired at George Mason University in 2001, and had I not been so fortunate as to join the team at CHNM, I never would have had the many opportunities I did to spend so much time thinking about, proposing, creating, and playing with digital media in history. Anyone who was ever fortunate enough to spend more than five minutes with Roy knows just how generous he was with his ideas, his time, and his encouragement. At the same time, Roy was never shy about pushing me (and everyone else he knew) to do a better job than we were currently doing. His incredibly untimely death shattered all who knew him, but we are so much the better for having known him. When I first proposed writing this book, he was my biggest supporter. That I never had his sage advice and careful, incisive critique during the writing process means this book is not nearly what it could have been were Roy still with us.

Many others have encouraged me, offered useful suggestions along the way, and inspired me with their ideas and enthusiasm for the project. Among those I particularly want to thank for their help along the way are my colleagues Dan Cohen, Kelly Schrum, Tom Scheinfeldt, Brian Platt, and Jack Censer. Elsewhere in the digital history and historical pedagogy community, Stan Katz, Kevin Kee, Bill Turkel, David Pace, Randy Bass, Lendol Calder, Noralee Frankel, Robert Townsend, Sean Brawley, Susan Groundwater (who invited me to teach history to her fifth grade class), and everyone who ever helped make Zotero what it is, helped in various ways. A research leave from George Mason in 2010 made it possible to get a great deal of the research and writing done and a Pew National Fellowship from the Carnegie Foundation for the Advancement of Teaching kick-started my research in the scholarship of teaching and learning in history all the way back in 1999. None of these individuals or organizations can be held accountable for any shortcomings you may find here. That responsibility lies with me.

I want to thank Tom Dwyer at the University of Michigan Press, first for believing in this project, then for their help making the book better, and most of all, for sticking with me when I missed my initial deadline. I would also like to thank my copy editor at the University of Michigan Press, Jessica LeTourneur, who made me sound much more eloquent than I actually am.

None of the insights I've gained over the years about the intersection of history and digital media would have been possible without my students, first at the University of New Hampshire, then at Grinnell College, then at Texas Tech University, and finally at George Mason. Over the years they put up with my many and sometimes not-very-successful experiments with teaching and technology, told me what they thought in pretty frank terms, inspired me with their insights, good humor, great ideas, and willingness to try new things, even if they were pretty sure many of my ideas were loopy. It is commonplace in American education to complain that "students today" are not nearly as good as some mythical group of students "back in the day." I find that characterization of our students to be insulting, misinformed, and just plain intellectually lazy. I have tremendous respect for my students and all they have taught me over the years and would not trade them for anyone else's students anywhere.

Finally, I want to acknowledge the love and encouragement of my wife, Susan, and my sons Ross and Spencer Kelly. Even though they thought it regularly, never once did they say, "Aren't you done with that book yet?"

Contents

Introduction

The historian is of his own age, and is bound to it by the
conditions of human existence.
—E. H. Carr, What is History? (1962)

Everyone who teaches has had moments when students do, say, write,
or create something that causes us to think about teaching in new ways.
Sometimes it is only with hindsight that we realize just how profound the
effect was. Other times, what happens is so obvious that even if we try we
cannot ignore the impact it has on us. One such moment in my career as
a history teacher came several years ago in my Western Civilization course.
Despite all the thinking I had been doing on how digital media were transforming student learning about the past, that day I realized I had missed
a very significant change in the way my students thought about learning,
about the production of historical knowledge, and about the nature of
historical evidence.

   On that particular day we were winding up the Second World War
and my goal was to spend some quality time on the war crimes tribunals
at Nuremberg and Tokyo, both to demonstrate how the victorious powers
had decided to handle the resolution of the war differently than they had
in 1918, and to introduce my students to the ideas of human rights implicit
in the indictments for crimes against humanity. I had already given them
several primary sources—copies of the indictments at Nuremberg, the
Universal Declaration of Human Rights—and I came to class armed with
links to newsreel footage of the Nuremberg prosecutions that were available on YouTube. The students' first task was to discuss the primary sources

among themselves. Then we watched the video clips as a precursor to a general class discussion of the questions I had given them. In one of the clips a van pulled up in front of the courtroom and the voice-of-God narrator Ed Herlihy described the scene in a combination of triumphal and apocalyptic prose.[1] When the clip ended, one of my students objected to the background music, saying that it reminded him too much of some of the Nazi propaganda film clips we'd watched the previous week, largely excerpts from Leni Riefenstahl's *Triumph of the Will*. Several of the students nodded agreement with him and so we paused for a few minutes to discuss propaganda in general, how it might be similar or different across cultures, and how the makers of newsreels might be working with a limited number of possible clips on short notice. We also spent a few more minutes discussing how music changes the feel of a documentary and how documentary films—whether newsreels or otherwise—are constructed versions of reality. I was pleased with the discussion because it engaged a number of the students in the room and helped to set up some other points I planned to make toward the end of the semester about media and historical knowledge. In short, I left class that day feeling like it had been a good day.

The following class session was not at all what I expected. My plan for the day was to work on our analysis of the beginning of the Cold War and the first stages of European integration. Instead, I was knocked off course even before class began. One of my students came up to me while I was arranging my laptop and told me he had "fixed" the Nuremberg video we watched during the previous class session. Fixed? When I asked what he meant by "fixed" he handed me his thumb drive and told me to start with the first file in the folder marked Nuremberg. So, once everyone had settled themselves, I told the class what was going on and launched the first file I found. It was the same Universal Newsreels video we had watched the prior class, but my student had stripped out much of the music track and substituted new background music. As soon as we heard the ominous bass notes from the movie *Jaws* we all chuckled at his joke. Then he told me to open the second file. This time he had replaced the triumphalist music of the original with passages from Mozart's *Requiem*. As he then explained, Mozart's music was much more appropriate to the seriousness of the situation being shown in the film and so, "From now on, Professor Kelly, you should use my version." Not surprisingly, I responded that as much as I might prefer his remix, it wasn't the original source. He shrugged his shoulders and said, "Yeah, but mine's better." When I saw that perhaps half the class was on his side, I gave up on the Cold War and European integration and spent the rest of class in a vain attempt to win the class back over to my side of the historian's fence. The vast majority of the students agreed with me that original sources were original sources and that, in general, they were preferred to mashed-up or remixed sources. But even after a very animated discussion of historical evidence, a significant number—perhaps as many as half—still felt that his version was better and so I probably should use it from now on.

For more than a decade I have been making the not-especially-original argument that digital technology—particularly, but not limited to, the Internet—is transforming the ways in which students are learning about the past.[2] But the more I have thought about what went on in that Western Civilization class several years ago, the more I have come to realize that something much bigger and more consequential has already happened. Moreover, I am convinced that the future of history teaching depends on our ability and willingness to accommodate ourselves to the rapidly accelerating, technology-driven cycle of change that is transforming the teaching, learning, research, and production of historical knowledge. For more than a century, historians have been able to shrug off demands for changes in how we teach our subject and most of us have remained stubbornly ignorant of the history of teaching and learning in our discipline. Unfortunately, no matter what we might like to believe, from the end of the Second World War until the late 1990s, there really has been almost no significant innovation in the methods of history teaching. Teaching history through primary sources rather than through textbooks? That "innovation" dates from the last two decades of the nineteenth century.[3] How about "problem-based learning"? Alas for us, that "innovation"—all the rage at the moment—first appeared in history classrooms in the first decade of the twentieth century.[4] To be sure, we have been very innovative when it comes to the topics in history we study and teach about, but when it comes to teaching methods in history, until recently there hasn't been much new under the sun. As the example of my student's Nuremberg remix indicates, we should be very worried that we are losing the rising generation of students because our approach to the past seems increasingly out of sync with their heavily intermediated lives.

Let's be clear—my student's remix of that newsreel signified was not just a playful approach to the past. He was also demonstrating concrete evidence of a way of thinking about the nature of evidence and how evidence can and should be used to make sense of past events. As I first wrote these words in the spring of 2010, the novel *Axolotl Roadkill* by seventeen-year-old German author Helene Hegemann sat in the number-two position on the hardcover fiction best-seller list of the magazine *Der Spiegel.* Much to the outrage of critics (most of whom were significantly older than seventeen), Hegemann freely admitted lifting substantial portions of her book from the work of other authors without any attribution. Hegemann called this remix of other authors' work legitimate because, as she said in a formal statement via her publisher, "There's no such thing as originality anyway, just authenticity."[5] Following her line of argument, the remixed version of that Nuremberg newsreel was a more authentic source, at least in my student's eyes, which helps to explain why I had such a difficult time convincing the class that I should not use it when teaching about Nuremberg.

My student was making history out of factual evidence in ways that a number of prominent historians over the years have advocated.[6] To be sure, he was altering a primary source to make a point about the past, but it is worth considering two things: to what degree was his alteration of the source to make a point substantially different from, say, a historian's decision to crop an image so it will fit neatly into the point he or she is trying to make in class? Certainly my student's decision was much closer to that of photographer Roger Fenton's staging of photographs taken in the Valley of the Shadow of Death during the Crimean War in late April 1855, or Alexander Gardner's similarly staged photographs from the American Civil War.[7] History abounds with fakery and forgeries like Fenton's and Gardner's, and one of the tasks of the historian is to uncover such alterations of the historical record if it is possible. But history also abounds with a more subtle problem—facts played up or played down by storytellers, chroniclers, journalists, and historians to make a point they want to make. I submit that my student altered that source to make a historical argument—something we lament the absence of in so much of our students' work—and while I wish he could have made the argument without altering a source, I also recognize that his act of history making lies somewhere between the deliberate forgeries of Fenton and Gardner and the severe injunctions of Leopold von Ranke demanding that history be told as it actually was. One of the main purposes of this book is to explore the gray areas that acts like my student's open up in hopes of helping us think about what history may become in the digital age.

What then is a historian to do in the face of students who may be more interested in authenticity than originality? First and foremost we have to set aside our squeamishness, if only so we can examine those feelings for what they are. I will admit to having had to force myself to do just that over the past several years. After all, I am a firm believer that history is built upon a foundation of evidence—evidence drawn from primary sources in as close to their original state as can be accessed. Any remixing of those sources makes me more than a little squeamish: it makes me downright uncomfortable, just as I imagine many art critics in Vienna felt when Gustav Klimt unveiled his *Medicine* mural in the Assembly Hall of the University of Vienna more than 100 years ago. Klimt's work was so far outside their understanding of what constituted art or beauty that most of those critics had difficulty finding a way to describe the work and simply rejected it out of hand, with many decrying it as an obscenity. While we do not, or at least should not, expect our students to establish new ways of making sense of the past that are as groundbreaking as Klimt's work, it seems to me that it is incumbent on us to give them enough free rein to experiment and to accept the results of those experiments as worthy of consideration as history. In fact, one of the main arguments in this book is that by giving students the freedom to experiment, to play with the past in new and creative ways, whether using digital media or not, we not only open ourselves up to the possibility that they can do very worthy and interesting historical work, but also that there are significant learning gains that result from giving students that freedom. When students work on topics they are interested in, in ways that make sense to them, the level of their engagement not only with the assignment, but also with the fundamental historical assumptions that the assignment raises, certainly goes up.

I am not arguing that students should be free to do whatever they want, however they want—quite the contrary, in fact. I am, however, arguing that by structuring learning opportunities that address fundamental historical problems and give students enough free rein to take real ownership of their work, we open ourselves (and them) up to the possibility that much more can happen in our courses than the development of the most basic skills of historical analysis. At the same time, I argue that we do not have a great deal of time when it comes to making the transition to new ways of teaching and learning that are grounded in the potentialities of digital media. Thomas Kuhn introduced us to the idea that when existing and accepted paradigms no longer suffice to answer pressing scientific questions, first a crisis and then a revolution occurs, leading to new ways of thinking about old problems.[8] Historians are more fortunate than physicists, because we are experiencing no such obvious crisis. In fact, as a discipline, we seem fairly well pleased with ourselves when it comes to the state of historical research and analysis, and many of us remain generally dismissive of the value of new media technologies for the teaching and learning of our discipline.[9] But we ignore the revolution going on all around us at our peril.

While Helene Hegemann's notions of originality and authenticity might seem easy to dismiss as a passing fad of the young, it is not so easy to dismiss the work of award-winning Canadian environmental and digital historian William Turkel on "interactive ambient and tangible devices for knowledge mobilization." Turkel argues that "As academic researchers we have tended to emphasize opportunities for dissemination that require our audience to be passive, focused and isolated from one another and from their surroundings. We need to supplement that model by building some of our research findings into communicative devices that are transparently easy to use, provide ambient feedback, and are closely coupled with the surrounding environment."[10] Turkel, the historian's ambassador to the "maker" movement, further advocates the use of new digital devices to fabricate objects from the past in real time as a way to give students access to the three-dimensional look and feel of historical objects.[11] In other words, in Turkel's view, historical knowledge and analysis can become tactile, not as a replacement for other forms of the representation of knowledge, but as another way to give students of history access to insights about the past. For example, historians and art historians have written many books and articles about the graffiti decorating buildings and other structures around the world over the many centuries. Students of the past can view those images on the page or the screen and can read the historian's analysis of the images; the cultures within which they were produced; and the biographies of the artists, if the artists are known. At a conference in 2010, Turkel and I used a digital camera, off-the-shelf image-manipulation software, and a device called a Craft ROBO, to reproduce a graffiti stencil I photographed on a street corner in Vienna, Austria, in 2008.[12] With the stencil we made and a can of spray paint, we could have (but did not) gone around town tagging buildings with that Austrian stencil. We would not have been recreating the historical object I photographed in 2008, but we would have been reenacting, in an authentic way, the process by which that Austrian stencil was used by whomever tagged the building I photographed two years earlier, thereby at least opening up the possibility that we might have gained some new or different insights into what it was like to be a public artist in the Austrian capital. Of late, cognitive psychologists have called into question the empirical basis for claims that students have different "learning styles," but those same studies do point to strong evidence for learning gains accruing from students encountering evidence, problems, and analysis from multiple perspectives.[13] Had Turkel and I gone about tagging local buildings with that stencil we created, the tactile nature of that experience would certainly have fallen into the category of a different perspective on the past.

You would be well within your rights if Turkel's tactile approaches to the past sound like they are a long way from writing a book or a scholarly article. He, and those working with him, represent just one variant of serious historical investigation that bears almost no resemblance to the work we have done for more than a century. "Interactive ambient and tangible devices for knowledge mobilization" have almost nothing to do with the forms of historical scholarship we have grown comfortable with—or even with primary sources as we know them. Turkel is not alone. My colleague Dan Cohen, director of the Center for History and New Media, recently launched a new version of the historical journal. *Digital Humanities Now* uses an algorithm to scrape content from the Internet (blogs, websites, social media) and then editors decide which items to feature on the journal's home page. Content gathered by the algorithm includes blog posts, updates to historical wikis, new content from selected Twitter feeds, and other forms of rapidly changing information about the digital humanities. Because the content on the home page changes daily (and more often, in the case of the river of unfiltered content also summarized on the site), readers get a real-time view of what is happening in the digital humanities.[14] The fact that serious historians like Turkel and Cohen—among others—are doing this sort of work is a harbinger of the sort of change we can expect in our discipline. If new media are changing our discipline, then how can the teaching and learning of our discipline not change as well? In his essay "Historical Thinking and Other Unnatural Acts," Sam Wineburg argues, "the essence of achieving mature historical thought rests precisely on our ability to navigate the jagged landscape of history, to traverse the terrain that lies between the poles of familiarity with and distance from the past." I submit that somewhere between Leopold von Ranke and Helene Hegemann lies a similarly jagged landscape of history, and scholars like Turkel and his colleagues in the Lab for Humanistic Fabrication, Cohen, and my colleagues at the Center for History and New Media will be the ones to help us traverse that landscape. My hope is that this book will help readers negotiate those parts of that landscape that have to do with teaching and learning.

The task I have set for myself is a bit daunting, especially given how entrenched notions about how history ought to be taught are among those who teach history. One reason these notions are so powerful is that for more than 100 years historians have been teaching their courses much the same way.[15] The typical high school or college history class is dominated by lectures aimed at imparting a mix of facts and analysis to students who are expected to dutifully listen, take notes, study that information, and then demonstrate their mastery of the material either in essays (if the class is small enough) or in exams. History is not alone as a discipline that relies upon lectures as the primary mode of instruction. We are also not alone in ignoring the fact—demonstrated again and again in studies of student cognition—that lecturing to/at students is among the worst possible ways to teach them anything.[16] Even in lecture courses carefully designed to maximize student recall of factual information, most students retain only about 20 percent of what was taught to them in lectures.[17] Moreover, after twenty minutes of being lectured to, most students report that their minds have wandered at least once from the subject at hand (and this finding comes from before the days when students brought laptops, cell phones, and iPods to class). Even in those classes where time is set aside for discussion on a regular basis, researchers who study such things find that the majority of questions asked by instructors across the disciplines focus on the recall of factual information. Recalling factual information on an exam is not, by any definition, the kind of real learning that leads to higher order thinking about complex ideas, nor is it in any way a sign of what we like to call "historical thinking." Writing about the past is one way students acquire and demonstrate the higher order thinking we are hoping to teach. The skills of analysis students demonstrate in writing one five-page paper after another is not something to be scoffed at, and is, moreover, a set of skills that employers value. However, analytical writing is only one of the many ways students can advance both their knowledge of the past and their analytical skills.

One reason historians seem to feel it is so necessary to present students with so much factual information is that we know in our hearts that students cannot be expected to engage in sophisticated analysis of historical events unless they know what those historical events actually were. Because most college history curricula have dispensed with prerequisites for most courses, it is very difficult to assume that students arrive in class on day one knowing anything about the subject of our courses, and so we feel honor bound to start somewhere near the beginning of our subject—not all the way back to humanoids wandering out of Olduvai Gorge—but back a good way nevertheless, so that our students will have some sense of what led up to the events that will be focused on for the rest of the semester. But, because those prior events are less central to the main subject of the course, we often knock them all off in a couple of lectures. Imagine trying to take differential equations without first having taken calculus, but having a nice professor who spends the first week reviewing algebra, geometry, and then calculus before diving into the heavy lifting of the rest of the semester— that is what that first week of rapid review of the prior century (or three) must seem like to many of our students. Once we have told them what happened before the course began, then we make sure to tell them what happened during the time frame of the course itself. The time constraints of the ten-week quarter or the fourteen-week semester mean that even in the smallest class of students efficiency seems to dictate a certain amount of lecturing—or, as we often put it—"covering" the main events. But as Lendol Calder so cogently pointed out several years ago, "cover" can also mean to obscure or hide from view.[18] Thus, if we want to uncover what is really important in our courses, it seems clear that we need to give up on lecturing as the primary mode of historical instruction. How might that be possible in classes with 50, 100, 200, or even 500 students?[19] As we will see, digital technology offers us a way forward that makes it possible for our students to uncover important insights, no matter how many other students there are in our courses. It is worth noting that students are not unaware that listening to lectures and taking notes are not the best ways to learn. Is it any wonder then, that at a moment in time where they can suddenly access more information about any topic than they can possibly use or make sense of, that more and more students have lost patience with us and our teaching methods and have either shut down—choosing the path of least resistance to a grade they want—or have begun to make sense of the past in ways that seem as foreign to us as the remix of the Nuremberg newsreel did to me?

It is likely that even if you agree with some of my argument(s), you may be thinking, "Ah, but his critique doesn't apply to me." After all, you may lecture no more than a few times in an entire semester and your classes may be built around a series of learning exercises that emphasize active learning, community-engaged learning, problem-based learning, or other teaching methods demonstrated to engender the kinds of historical thinking almost all of us say we strive for with our students. If that is the case, you are in a very small minority. Study after study turns up the same data; namely, that between 75 and 90 percent of college instructors in courses not designated as seminars rely upon lecturing as the primary mode of instruction in their courses. While most historians I know claim that they make the analysis of primary source materials a central feature of their courses, a reasonably recent analysis of college history syllabi by Dan Cohen indicates that in introductory American history surveys, a substantial fraction of college faculty assign no book other than the textbook, and that only a small number assigned the primary source reader tied to the textbook.[20] Amazingly, at a time (2005) when millions of primary sources in American history were already online from reputable organizations such as the Library of Congress and the National Archives, only 6 percent of the 792 syllabi Cohen included in his study offered students links to online primary sources. A more recent study (2010) by Robert Townsend of the American Historical Association (AHA) indicates that in the five years since Cohen's article appeared, still fewer than half of the more than 4,000 teaching historians responding to an AHA survey regularly use online sources in their classes.[21] Anyone who has taught history in the past decade knows that the first, and often the only, place students of any age look for primary sources is online. When students look online almost exclusively, and fewer than half of their professors point them to online resources, we see another reason why students and their instructors are proceeding into the past on rapidly diverging tracks. No wonder students are teaching themselves what to do with those sources.

In 2000, it was possible for a scholar like Sarah Horton to argue that, "although moving your course materials onto the Web may not shake the foundations of Learning [sic], it is the first step to devising a Web teaching method."[22] Perhaps in 2000 it was also possible to write an entire book on "web teaching" that only "touches" (her word) on the effectiveness of using digital media to teach. That is not the case any longer. But in 2000, "the Web" was mostly about image and text availability. The world of the World Wide Web has changed radically in the past decade—not only because we now call it the Internet. When Horton was writing about how to teach with Internet resources, the resources she was talking about were websites created either by what we now call "legacy institutions"—that is, museums, libraries, and archives that pushed lots of content onto the Internet for users to view, or by teachers who likewise pushed content online, or created teaching exercises from that content that students were expected to use. The most interactive websites in 2000 were those that offered users access to discussion forums or, in rare cases, chat rooms where various topics could be discussed. But only a tiny fraction of Internet users had ever created content for the web beyond contributing to a discussion forum. In 2000 creating web content still required a fair amount of technical skill and the term "social network" had a completely different meaning than it does in today.

By contrast, the young people arriving on our campuses this fall have been creating content online for as long as they can remember. According to a Pew research study published in February 2010, 75 percent of Americans between the ages of 18 and 29—the "Millennials"—have created a personal profile on a social networking site such as Facebook, 62 percent have accessed the Internet away from home via a wireless connection, and one in five has posted video of themselves online on a site like YouTube. When the 18–29 cohort is broken down into subgroups of 18–24 and 25–29 years old, the percentage of those using social media rises to 81 percent.[23] College students are even more aggressive adopters of Internet sites where the user creates the content rather than simply consuming content; they use the Internet in active, not passive ways. In the fall of 2005, 85 percent of freshmen at the University of North Carolina-Chapel Hill had a Facebook account at the beginning of the semester, and by the end of their first semester 94 percent had such an account.[24] It is worth noting that in 2005 the use of such social media by students was still relatively new. It seems safe to assume, therefore, that by 2010, when the number of Facebook users worldwide has surpassed 700 million, the percentage of incoming freshmen who already have a profile on one or more social networking sites is substantially greater than the 85 percent found at UNC six years ago. By contrast, the Pew Research Center report found that in the next generational cohort—the so-called Gen X, now 30–45 years old—only 50 percent had an online profile on a social networking site, and only 6 percent had posted video of themselves online.

As these data make abundantly clear, not only is the Internet of 2012 radically different than the Internet of 2000, but more importantly, students' use of digital media is substantially different. They still consume a great deal of online content, but just as important, if not more important, they are aggressive creators of online content as well. As a recent report from the Massachusetts Institute of Technology (MIT) on young people and technology argues, "The growing availability of digital media-production tools, combined with sites where young people can post and discuss media works, has created a new media ecology that supports everyday media creation and sharing for kids engaged in creative production."[25] Thus, the second central argument of this book is that any use of digital media for teaching and learning that does not take into account this shift from consumer to creator is problematic from the start. Throughout this book, I suggest various ways we can capitalize on this creative impulse of our students to make the past more exciting and more relevant to them, not only in the classes they are taking, but also in the lives they have planned for themselves. By structuring our teaching and their learning about the past around ways that digital technology now promotes active engagement with, rather than passive acquisition (and reading) of historical content, we will be creating learning opportunities for our students that have a much higher likelihood of producing the learning gains we hope for when we teach. Instead of asking them to sit, listen, and record what we say—a teaching strategy that cognitive science has demonstrated quite conclusively to be unproductive—we can now ask our students to do what we do: make history out of the raw material of the past.

The goal of this book is to challenge historians, but also others teaching in the humanities and social sciences, to think carefully about the ways that digital media are changing teaching and learning in our fields in the face of changes such as those mentioned earlier. At its most challenging, this book considers how the remix culture developing around and through new media is making it possible for our students (and us) to produce either new knowledge about the past, or old knowledge presented in new ways. Even though we may not be able to anticipate the results of our students' work in the digital age, it remains incumbent upon us to guide them through the past, and through the ways digital technology might be used to understand and represent the past. After all, the values of the professional historian do not change just because the medium changes. To help with that task, chapter 1 provides an overview of several decades' worth of research on how students learn about the past, which sets the stage for a discussion and analysis of how students search for, and find, historical content. Subsequent chapters consider how students might actually analyze historical sources that now rain down on them, not by their dozens or hundreds, but by their millions or hundreds of millions—a problem of abundance that will only increase with each passing year. Once they have analyzed the historical data they acquire, our students have to do something with that data, and so the last portion of this book considers ways in which students can, and slowly but surely are, already creating new forms of historical knowledge. It is always risky for historians to write about the future—after all, we still know far too little about the past—but my hope is that by challenging the reader to think hard about the future of teaching and learning in the digital age, every reader will find at least one new way to think about both the past and the future in our discipline. Moreover, I hope to convince the reader that my two central arguments—that we should use digital media to create active learning opportunities wherein our students create content online, and that we should be open to the surprising results our students may come up with when they create that content—are worth taking seriously.

$\langle$ 1 $\rangle$

Thinking

How Students Learn About the Past

How do students think about the past? For more than a century historians
have been pondering this question, both in terms of what facts about the
past our students ought to know, and just how it is they make sense—or
try to make sense—of historical information. While the study of student
thinking about the past has not been one of the major fields of endeavor
among historians, that does not mean the issue has been ignored altogether. Toward the end of the last century the teaching of history in both
colleges and schools was undergoing a process of professionalization and
this process spawned a number of how-to books aimed at the teacher who
was now expected to devote the bulk of his or her effort to one subject—
history. The great concern of this prescriptive literature was, not surprisingly, how best to teach students about the past so that they might become
better citizens of their country—a goal that has not changed much, at least
with respect to history teaching in the schools.[1] Most of what we find in
these studies from the late nineteenth and early twentieth centuries was
instruction on how best to teach history rather than any concern with how
students learn history, but that does not mean that the authors of such
books and articles were unaware of the fact that an understanding of how
students learn is essential to any approach to teaching.

For instance, in 1897 Burke Hinsdale opined, "In dealing with the history of a country or nation, the first thing to be done is to fix in the pupil's
mind firmly the main points—an outline—a framework—in which he can
dispose and arrange minor facts and details as he requires them . . . ," and,

14

"A memory that lays hold of subject-matter should be stimulated rather than a mere verbal memory."[2] Hinsdale also recognized that lecturing at students, especially beginning students, was not the most effective method of teaching: "The lecture is not the proper vehicle for conveying elementary knowledge of history. Experience often shows that courses of lectures that have been taken with interest and are recalled with pleasure, have left little behind them save mistaken notions and vague ideas."[3] It is a bit disheartening to realize that more than 100 years ago historians were already warning their peers about the problems of lecturing (fig. 1).

In 1906, Charles Homer Haskins, one of the great historians of his day, chaired a committee of the American Historical Association charged with examining how best to teach history to college students. Haskins's report begins: "The most difficult question which now confronts the college teacher of history seems, by general agreement, to be the first year of the college course."[4] Haskins and his colleagues came to this conclusion because, in their view, the first year of the college course in history required students to spend too much time in lectures that offered up too much factual information for any student to take in, much less make sense of. Ironically, given the typical university history curriculum in 2011, the Haskins report concluded that freshmen ought to be taught history in small seminars more focused on the close reading of historical evidence, and only in their final year of college should they be expected to take a grand survey of a historical subject, because it was only after they had learned the methods of the historian that they could be expected to successfully synthesize important facts from lectures on topics such as Western Civilization. In 1917, J. Carleton Bell described the ways that students acquired something he called "the historic sense." According to Bell, only some students were successful in achieving this "sense," which included "great skill in the orderly arrangement of their historical data, skill in seizing upon essential points of the narrative and keeping these well in the foreground of their thinking, skill in massing minor considerations to support their main positions."[5] Too many other students, he wrote, "take all statements with equal emphasis, keep all parts of the discussion upon the same level, and become hopelessly confused by the multiplicity of details."[6] If Bell's description of his students from 1917 sounds much like descriptions we often hear (or purvey) of our own students, at least some blame should lie in the fact that our teaching methods have not changed much since 1917.[7]

Two distinct areas of concern emerged from those earliest specula-

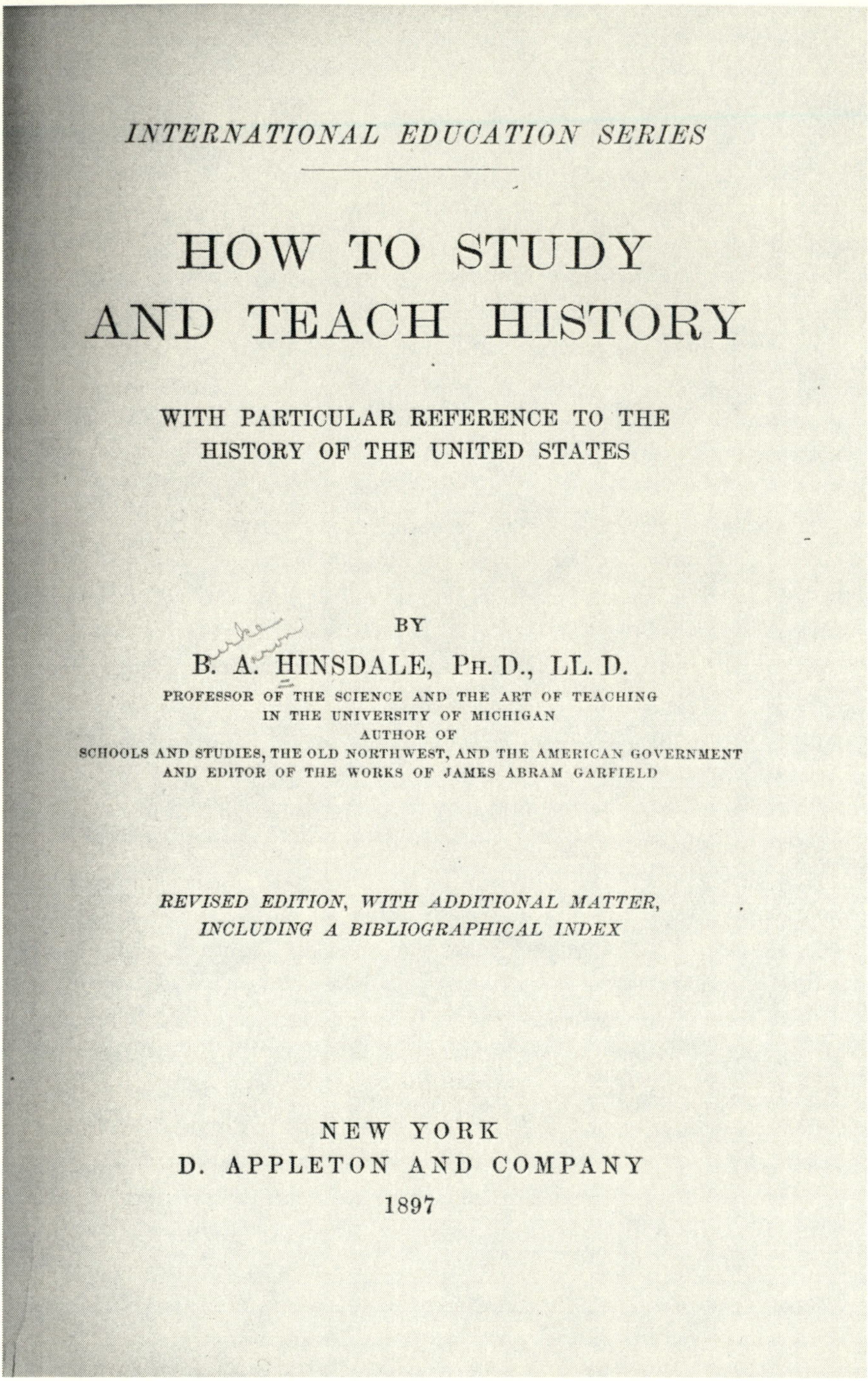

INTERNATIONAL EDUCATION SERIES

HOW TO STUDY
AND TEACH HISTORY

WITH PARTICULAR REFERENCE TO THE
HISTORY OF THE UNITED STATES

BY

B. A. HINSDALE, Ph. D., LL. D.

PROFESSOR OF THE SCIENCE AND THE ART OF TEACHING
IN THE UNIVERSITY OF MICHIGAN
AUTHOR OF
SCHOOLS AND STUDIES, THE OLD NORTHWEST, AND THE AMERICAN GOVERNMENT
AND EDITOR OF THE WORKS OF JAMES ABRAM GARFIELD

REVISED EDITION, WITH ADDITIONAL MATTER,
INCLUDING A BIBLIOGRAPHICAL INDEX

NEW YORK
D. APPLETON AND COMPANY
1897

Fig. 1. Title page of *How to Study And Teach History: With Particular Reference to the History of the United States* (New York: D. Appleton and Company, 1894) by B. A. Hinsdale.

tions about how best to teach history: content knowledge and procedural knowledge. In the wider public debates about what students ought to know about the past, it is content knowledge that most animates these discussions.[8] Among the best-known American examples of the arguments over what students ought or ought not be taught in history classes came during the controversy that arose over the proposed national standards for the teaching and learning of American history in early 1995. Slade Gorton, a freshman senator from Washington state, asked his colleagues, "Mr. President, what is a more important part of our Nation's history for our children to study—George Washington or Bart Simpson?"[9] Gorton's angst over (and oversimplification of) the proposed standards for history education in the United States reflected a profound and widespread concern about what American children ought to know about the past. Without the correct understanding of the nation's past, the argument goes, our children cannot become the kinds of citizens we want and need for the future of our country (whichever country that might be). But in these debates factual knowledge is often conflated with correct understanding—we assume that if our children know the facts, they will understand the facts. As Stéphane Lévesque points out, such fulminating about what ought to be taught and not taught is really a battle over the contested space of memory—memory that is, as Pierre Nora argues "absolute, [while] history is always relative."[10] The notion of history as always relative, something historians are quite comfortable with, can have quite the opposite effect on those debating what ought to and ought not to be taught. Perhaps the most straightforward recent statement of the just-the-facts view of history is a law passed by the Florida legislature in 2006.

> American history shall be viewed as factual, not constructed, shall be viewed as knowable, teachable, and testable, and shall be defined as the creation of a new nation based largely on the universal principles stated in the Declaration of Independence.[11]

It is fashionable among historians to put popular debates over the teaching of content knowledge into an ideological frame.[12] Such claims ignore the fact that all sides in debates over which facts to teach generally proceed from much the same view of history teaching; namely, that students ought to be taught the correct/important/essential facts about the past and that any consideration of historical methods or analysis is secondary to the acquisition of the proper set of the facts. In the debates over content, there is generally little popular disagreement over what history is—the debate is most typically over whether to teach "our" set of facts, or "yours."[13] The "ours/yours" debate takes on such great urgency because we tend to believe that history serves a very important function in the process of nation building. While all sides in the debate over what ought to be taught generally agree on this point, it is the definition of the nation being built that is at issue. For instance, is the history of the nation the history of all the groups living in the state, or are so-called marginal groups (however such groups might be defined) so marginal that they are of only secondary importance to the narrative of who we are? What great moral lessons can we learn from our past that will guide us in the future? Are those lessons the ones taught to us by the leaders of the nation way back when, or are the more important lessons to be found in the day-to-day struggles of the working classes who built the state through their toil?[14] Whichever side is speaking up about which facts ought to be taught at any particular moment, their spokespeople are fond of wringing their hands and worrying that "kids today" just don't know much about history because they perform below expectations on standardized tests designed to gauge their retention of facts.[15]

This view of history teaching as the communication of a specific body of factual knowledge to students is one that also resonates with many, if not most, history students. As Robert Bain points out, many students come to the history classroom with the following view of their subject: "The past is filled with facts, historians retrieve those facts, students memorize the facts, and all this somehow improves the present."[16] Knowing facts about the past so the present can be improved is especially important to many students because they also believe that history regularly repeats itself—so if we just pay close attention to what happened in the past, we will know what to expect in the future and can avoid making some of those same darned mistakes our parents, grandparents, and great-grandparents made. Another challenge history teachers face when it comes to what students think history is all about, is students' tendency to believe that they already know and understand people in the past. This belief in the familiarity of the past, if tested, often leads to some interesting responses in the classroom. For instance, when I teach about the female suffrage movement at the *fin-de-siècle,* my students are often disbelieving when I give them evidence of anti-suffrage demonstrations at which hundreds, and sometimes thousands, of women attended to express their opposition to being given the vote.[17] "Of course every woman would want the vote," my students' thinking goes, and if they are correct, then the logical conclusion is that the sources I give them must be wrong. These sorts of exercises create a tension in students' minds between the familiar and the strange and are very difficult to get right. We want to destabilize their assumptions about the past without making the past so strange, so other, that they write it off as either too weird or simply impossible to make sense of.[18] Instead, if students are forced to grapple with historical evidence on its own terms, not based on stereotypes they bring to that analysis, they then begin to question the broad generalizations they love to make about "women," or "Nazis," or the "Chinese."[19] Writing about drama rather than history, Bertold Brecht calls this breaking free of deeply held stereotypes "alienating the familiar."[20] Sam Wineburg demonstrates the difficulties of alienating the familiar very clearly in his essay "Making (Historical) Sense in the New Millennium." In his interviews with high school history students and their parents, Wineburg found that when it came to the past, his subjects demonstrated signs of both collective memory and what he calls "collective occlusion."[21] Perhaps the most striking example of collective occlusion that he offers is what happened when he showed a young woman a photograph of construction workers demonstrating in favor of the Vietnam War. When asked what was happening in the photograph, the student replied that she was looking at a photograph of an anti-war demonstration, despite clear evidence in the image to the contrary. Wineburg concludes that the narrative of those Americans who were pro-war has been occluded by the much stronger narrative of the anti-war movement, to the point where students will cling so firmly to their belief in the dominant narrative that they will ignore clear evidence that contradicts what they believe.

Even when we are successful in convincing students that the past is indeed a foreign country that they can peek into, but can't actually visit, they are still likely to assume that they know people from that foreign country anyway. James Axtell calls this predilection a case of students assuming *self*-knowledge is akin to *historical*-knowledge, by which he means that they assume that because they are women or Republicans or whatever, they have unique insights into how women or Republicans 100 years ago thought and acted.[22] Getting them to set aside these assumptions is more than a little difficult and sometimes impossible, because these assumptions are grounded in our basic beliefs about ourselves. As Wineburg says, "The familiar past entices us with the promise that we can locate our own place in the stream of time and solidify our identity in the present."[23] We want the past to be knowable through the lens of our own experiences.[24] History is not alone in facing this difficulty when it comes to teaching students about that which is unfamiliar, foreign, or seemingly counterintuitive. As Carl Wieman and Kathleen Perkins have found, our students' reliance on folk wisdom, is just as difficult to break down in physics as it is in history.[25]

A powerful demonstration of the simple solutions students often offer to complex historical problems can be seen in a video clip from an interview with a student named Chuck on the website Historical Thinking Matters. In this example, the student was given two American newspaper stories about the outbreak of the Spanish-American War—one that states unequivocally that the Spanish were responsible for the sinking of the battleship *Maine*, and one that says the cause of the *Maine*'s explosion remains unclear. Chuck, however, has almost no uncertainty: "It was blown up by the Spanish because we then had a war with them. So if there was a Spanish-American War and this happened right before it, then this is probably what started [the war]."[26] For whatever reason, Chuck's existing narratives of the American past, combined with an analytical strategy founded on straightforward common sense, brought him to his firm conclusion about the sinking of the *Maine*.[27] This sort of analytical strategy is not limited to history students. In Wieman and Perkins' research, students were given a lecture on the physics of sound and then were given a demonstration of how sounds are created by a violin. Fifteen minutes later, only 10 percent of the students gave the correct answer from a list of four choices, defaulting instead to folk wisdom about how sound is produced.[28] As researchers such as Wineburg and Wieman have shown, breaking through these assumptions and analytical strategies is quite difficult, but as educators it is incumbent upon us to try.

Almost any historian will tell you that the "facts first" view of history is one that is very different from the disciplinary thinking that we hope to inculcate in our students.[29] What then do historians mean when we talk about the study of history, if not the acquisition of a body of factual content? Before we decide, it is probably a good idea to stipulate what historians *do not* mean; namely, that facts do not matter. Historians, at least every historian I know, care passionately about facts supported by evidence. We know that all good history is built upon a foundation of evidence gleaned from as wide a variety of sources as can be obtained and verified. But facts from the past are not history.[30] History is a way of thinking, a way of knowing, a habit of mind. It is, as Robert Bain argues, an "epistemic activity."[31]

What then do historians mean by "historical thinking?" In 1971, Paul Ward, the executive secretary of the American Historical Association, described historical thinking.

> First accenting and clarifying the separate pieces of evidence; second, seeing how well the assembled evidence tells the story and explains the whole situation; and third, highlighting the human dimension in the evidence. Within the first grouping at least three main requirements are to be singled out: putting proper stress on the evidence, seeking illuminating comparisons, and critically evaluating the sources of information.[32]

While few historians would disagree with Ward that these are all important activities when it comes to thinking about the past, few today would see this list as sufficient to describe the complex activity we call historical thinking. Ward's definition emphasizes the mastering the evidence by putting it in its proper place in the larger picture of the past and betrays a devotion to the empiricist tradition that demands that historical evidence not be made to say anything more or less than it says.[33] Analysis of the evidence takes a backseat in this definition, and "highlighting the human dimension in the evidence" points to a need for students to attempt to establish an empathetic connection with those in the past—something that is often problematic when we are trying to encourage students to be more analytical. In the decades since, a more positivist view of history has taken hold among a wide swath of the historical community. For example, Stéphane Lévesque offers a definition of historical thinking that is much more focused on history as an epistemology rather than a craft.

> Historical thinking is, indeed, far more sophisticated and demanding than mastering substantive (content) knowledge, in that it requires the acquisition of such knowledge to understand the procedures employed to investigate its aspects and conflicting meanings . . . To think historically is thus to understand how knowledge has been constructed and what it means. Without such sophisticated insight into ideas, peoples, and actions, it becomes impossible to adjudicate between competing versions (and visions) of the past.[34]

Wineburg's view, already discussed in the introduction, is that:

> The argument I make pivots on a tension that underlies every encounter with the past: the tension between the familiar and the strange, between feelings of proximity and feelings of distance in relation to the people we seek to understand. Neither of these extremes does justice to history's complexity, and veering to one side or the other dulls history's jagged edges and leaves us with cliché and caricature. Achieving mature historical thought depends precisely on our ability to navigate the uneven landscape of history, to traverse the rugged terrain that lies between the poles of familiarity and distance from the past.[35]

As popular as Wineburg's definition has become, and as appealing as it is, not all historians would agree that it sums up what it means to think historically. For one thing, Wineburg is almost obsessed with the degree to which students need to be able to engage in a meta-discourse with themselves about their own thinking. As important as it is for those attempting to understand the past to realize how their modes of thinking influence the results of that thinking, too much focus on the meta-discourse—whether between and among historians, or in our students' own heads—can obscure the still very important and fundamental skills that undergird the larger discourse.

What then, do we mean when we say we want students to think historically? A vague definition of historical thinking along the lines of the definition of pornography proposed by Supreme Court Justice Potter Stewart in 1964 ("I know it when I see it") is not sufficient for our purposes.[36] If we are going to create rich digital media experiences for our students, if we are going to teach them how to be historians in this digital age—or, at the least we are going to teach them how to think historically using digital media as well as old-fashioned analog resources—then we need to be much more specific about what it is we mean when we say "historical thinking."

Almost every historian has his or her own personal list of the characteristics of historical thinking, but abilities that come up again and again are:

1. The ability to tell the difference between a primary and a secondary source.
2. The ability to "source the source"; that is, figure out who created the source, when it was created, and so on.

3. The ability to obtain information about the authority of the source and to assess that authority in light of other evidence.
4. The ability to set sources in their proper chronological order and to understand why that ordering is important.
5. The ability to construct an original argument based upon evidence from various sources.
6. The ability to recognize the strangeness of the past without being put off by that strangeness.
7. The ability to make comparative judgments about evidence.
8. The ability to recognize what one does not or cannot know from the evidence at hand.
9. The ability to understand that events are understood differently by different people.
10. The ability to triangulate between and among sources.
11. The ability to ask probing questions—not just what happened, but why did it happen this way and why didn't it happen that way?
12. The ability to recognize the role of causality.
13. The ability to critique evidence both on its own terms and in terms of its value to a larger analytical project.
14. The ability to recognize lines of argument in historical thought.
15. The ability to present the past in clear ways, whether in writing or in other media, saying what can be said and not saying what cannot.

In contrast to this rather long list, students typically have a much more basic list of what they think historical thinking means. Their thinking about historical thinking is often framed as a set of questions, which the answers will provide them with greater certainty about the past:

1. What happened?
2. When did it happen?
3. Why did it happen?
4. Who was responsible?
5. And a corollary question: Will that be on the exam?

It should be no surprise that students' approach to historical thinking is so instrumental. After all, they now live in a world where the measurement of their academic abilities prior to arriving at college was heavily dependent on their ability to select the correct answer from several choices and then fill in a bubble on a scantron sheet. The mania for standardized testing, so evident in the United States at this writing, has had many results—some salutary, some not—but in the history classroom, what it has meant is that students have become very adept at answering questions about the past, but not so adept at asking the kinds of questions we think are important. Where our students want certainty about the past, and to find the correct answer, due to the nature of our training, historians come to the classroom filled with a sense of historical contingency, a belief that the past is almost always equivocal, and that the first order of business for us is to formulate good questions about that past that will lead us in productive directions. The result of the inevitable clash between our students' desire for certainty and our devotion to uncertainty is that many, if not most, students spend the semester trying to create certainties out of the uncertainties presented by their professor, while the professor often becomes increasingly frustrated by his or her students' inability or simply unwillingness to dig into the uncertainties.[37] Most students do not want to spend much time on Weinberg's jagged edges of the past, fearing that they might be injured there. And who can blame them?

It is common among history teachers to complain that too often our students produce versions of the past that are heavy on cliché and caricature. To describe the work product of our students in this way is to do most of them a disservice. The jagged edge of history is an uncomfortable and unsettling place, and because so much of our teaching is predicated upon lecturing at them, it is no wonder they rely so heavily on tropes that they know and the regurgitation of facts we emphasize from the front of the room. For instance, it is a comforting certainty for American students that in the Second World War, Americans were the good guys, and the Germans and Japanese were the bad guys. This notion is reinforced by many years of schooling, television, and other forms of popular media. But if we take our students out onto the jagged edges of the past, they may learn unsettling realities, such as the fact that during "the Good War" U.S. commanders fought long and hard to suppress the practice of mutilating Japanese war dead by American servicemen.[38] Familiar stories about the war reinforce the notion that our servicemen fought in honorable ways. The strange reality of the past is that some of those same men mutilated enemy war dead in ways that the popular imagination almost always attributes to the bad guys on the other side. Coming to grips with this sort of strange reality is central to the development a more mature historical consciousness and is, therefore, one of the more difficult lessons we have to teach our students for them to succeed in our classes.

If we are to take full advantage of the opportunities that digital media offer us to improve the teaching and learning of history, we need to be very clear to ourselves and to our students what we mean when we say "historical thinking," and then create rich learning opportunities for students that encourage them to see history as we see it. The best way to use digital media to teach them to see history as we see it is to create learning opportunities that make it possible for our students to *do* history—to practice it as we practice it—to help them *make* history, using their own creative impulses, rather than simply giving us what they hope is the correct answer to a question we have posed. Archival and library websites are wonderful resources for students, but they do little more than provide access to material previously difficult to gain access to. Unlike the traditional lecture/paper/exam model of history instruction, digital media offers the possibility of creating new, exciting ways for students to be historians as they learn about the past. But it is also important to remember that technology is never *the* answer to a teaching problem. It can be one of several answers to such a problem, or it can help us find new and better ways to lead students to worthwhile solutions to thorny historical problems. In the end, however, these media are just one more resource for us.

Finding

Search Engine–Dependent Learning

As recently as fifteen years ago, historians were trapped in what John McClymer calls a pedagogy of scarcity.[1] With only so many historical sources available for students to work with; that is, those in print and those available at whatever archive or library might be close-by, the scope of our teaching about the past was limited to that which our students could reasonably study. In my own teaching on the history of Eastern Europe (from Poland south to Bulgaria), the scarcity of available sources was particularly acute because only a tiny fraction of my students could read any of the languages of the region, and East European history is such a small corner of the historical profession that only a few document readers were available that offered sources in translation. As a result, I had to design my teaching around what was available. I could talk about other topics, could refer students to the paragraph or two in a textbook that dealt with this or that issue, and could even assign a good monograph or two on just about any topic they were interested in. But my students could not do much, if any, real historical research on a topic in East European history unless that issue or event in some way included Americans or British citizens or interests, and so was therefore covered in the English-language press or government documents. Were it not for the heroic efforts of my dissertation advisor to have more than two dozen important documents from the history of East European nationalism translated into English, my options as a teacher and my students' options as historians would have been even more limited than they were.

As anyone who has ever searched for historical information online knows, those days of scarcity are gone forever.[2] Today, a student searching for information on any historical topic will find more primary sources than he or she can possibly cope with, and if this student waits a day or two, the volume of available primary source information will have increased significantly. As Roy Rosenzweig warned in 2003, "historians need to be thinking simultaneously about how to research, write, and teach in a world of unheard-of historical abundance."[3] The magnitude of that abundance is all around us online. The American Memory Project at the Library of Congress now offers more than 15 million primary sources for anyone to use in their research. The online image database Flickr contains more than 4.5 billion photographs, and the Library of Congress has announced that it will begin archiving everything posted to Twitter—approximately 50 million tweets per day (over 18 billion per year if the traffic on that website does not increase).[4] These are but three examples of the almost unlimited supply of historical primary sources posted online. Are you interested in Karl Marx? The website Marxists.org offers virtually everything Karl Marx ever wrote, plus works from almost 600 other authors representing a total of more than 53,000 documents from the history of the political left.[5] How about the history of consumer culture in the United States? The *Ad*Access* database at the Duke University Library offers high-resolution images of more than 7,000 print advertisements for everything from airlines to televisions.[6] Do you need a high-quality image of a rare eighteenth- or nineteenth-century map? The David Rumsey Map Collection offers users access to more than 22,000 high-resolution scans of such maps—some of which are available online only at this website, and the Perry-Castañeda Library at the University of Texas offers an additional 11,000 map images on their website.[7]

What does this incredible abundance mean for historical pedagogy? The most important result of the changes this abundance brings to the history classroom is that we can no longer control the information students have access to. Our students are no longer forced to rely on what we assign to them as the essential sources of information for the problems posed in a course. Instead, they wander off into the digital forest looking for additional information that may help them answer a question we pose, write a paper, come to class prepared to discuss a topic, or just pursue a line of personal inquiry suggested by something that came up in class. George Landow—one of the most prolific early adopters of digital media for his courses in literature—says that when students pursue their own lines of inquiry, they embark on unmediated intellectual quests, free from the control of faculty, textbook publishers, or others who might have controlled their inquiries in prior years.[8] This freedom to inquire turns the traditional relationship between student and teacher on its head, because with essentially unlimited access to historical information—for good or ill—students are no longer dependent upon their teachers for access to information that was once doled out to them. Even if we assume that in prior decades, students could go to the library and browse the stacks as a means to pursuing their own lines of inquiry, now, those libraries—where so many historians found a home in their own student years—could not rival the abundance now available on students' computer screens. For example: a delimited Google search run on January 5, 2011, on the name "Abraham Lincoln" produced 7,540,000 websites; 1,670,000 images; 10,600 videos; 1,320,000 books; and 121,000 scholarly articles. A further search on Lincoln across the multiple databases of newspapers provided by ProQuest Historical Newspapers produces another 80,252 citations. Together these add up to 10,741,852 possible resources for a student interested in Lincoln, his life, and his career. By contrast, a similar search of the catalog of the Library of Congress produced 4,277 citations, and such a search in the catalog of my university's fairly small library produced 871. Even allowing for significant duplication in the Google search returns, it is clear that there is just too much information online to work with in a practical way at this moment in the life of the Internet, and this problem of abundance gets worse with each passing day.

Clearly no one, not even the most experienced Lincoln scholars, can make sense of all those sources, and I am not suggesting that our students do anything like that. In fact, my own research on students' use of the Internet indicates that most do not embark on anything so prosaic as an "intellectual quest" as Landow envisioned it. Instead, they are most likely to be quite instrumental in the ways that they search for, retrieve, and use historical information available online.[9] Regardless of how deeply they delve into the digital archive, what is clear, however, is that with each passing year they rely less and less on conventional sources of information provided to them by their instructors (just ask your bookstore manager how many students bother to purchase a textbook), and more and more on readily available (and increasingly free) sources of information online. This removal of hierarchical controls over information in the digital realm is called disintermediation, and it has profound implications for how we teach students about the past.[10] A simple example of how disintermediation has transformed an industry is airline travel. Two decades ago a significant majority of airline travelers relied on professional travel agents to find and book flights for them. Recent research on the travel industry shows that almost 60 percent of all airline flights are booked online, and that traditional travel agencies have been relegated to niche players—booking complicated multi-destination trips; arranging group travel; or catering to wealthy, older, or very frequent flyers.[11] Passengers booking straightforward trips, especially those who have grown up with the Internet, use traditional travel agencies less and less each year. While I do not expect the history teacher to go the way of the travel agent any time soon, disintermediation is now a reality in our industry, just as it is in the travel industry, and we cannot ignore it, no matter how much we might want to. Already, we see the results of our loss of control over the information our students use whenever one of our students turns in a paper citing sources that, upon closer inspection, make us wince and the student blush when we point out the deficiencies in those sources. Conversations about these "oops moments" abound at professional conferences and among colleagues over coffee, but only rarely do these conversations take into account the ways that disintermediation has already transformed our field.

Because we have largely left our students to their own devices when it comes to finding historical information online, they have had to draw their own conclusions about how to proceed. Along the way, and almost entirely on their own, they have learned some lessons.

Lesson 1—Google Makes College Easy

Several years ago, one of my responsibilities was to review the teaching of the postdoctoral fellows we had hired to help us deliver the introductory Western Civilization survey course. In this particular case, the subject for that day was the Holocaust in twentieth-century Europe. As the students drifted in and took their seats, a few acknowledged me, but most just ignored me. Back in the last few rows, near me, a young woman asked a young man sitting next to her what he had in the way of answers to the questions their professor had posed at the end of the previous class session. He reached into his backpack, pulled out a sheaf of papers with some highlighting on them, and said, "I'm all set." He then ticked off a couple of reasonable answers derived from the highlighted text on his papers. "Where did you get *that*?" the young woman asked him. With a big smile on his face, he said, "I typed some key words into Google, printed out a few of these, and I'm good to go." She nodded with a look of commiseration, and what I took to be disappointment, that she had not taken such an obvious step to prepare for class.

Lesson 2—If It's Not Digital, It Doesn't Exist

Until a few years ago, before our program grew too large, each of our master's students was required to enroll in at least one directed reading with a faculty member. We devised a reading list together, and then the students met with their professor throughout the semester to discuss those readings. During one of those sessions with a particularly bright student, I was surprised to find that he had not read two of the articles I had assigned. Up to that point he had been very diligent in his preparation for our sessions, and so when I asked him why he had not read the articles in question, he replied that he had not been able to locate them. This surprised me, so I asked where he had looked and he said, "JSTOR." When I pointed out that while the journal the articles appeared in was not available in the JSTOR database, but they were available on a shelf in the university library, he looked up surprised and apologized, admitting that he had not thought to look for the "analog" version.

Lesson 3—If It Looks Reasonable, It's Probably Fine

Production values matter when it comes to students' decisions about web content. The more reasonable, or the more familiar, content appears to students, the more likely they are to use it. Thus, a website with good production values is more likely to draw students (and most web users) than one that looks like it was created in the days of Netscape Composer—offering black text on a gray screen, no margins, and no graphics. Similarly, a website that fulfills the user's expectations in terms of its format or style, may well fool even the most sophisticated of web users, as was the case in 2008 when a faux student blog created by students in my course, Lying About the Past, tricked a number of history teachers and educational developers (discussed in detail in chapter 5).[12]

Lesson 4—All Content Online Is Fair Game

When we think about students' search for information online, our focus is almost always on the things we know and are already familiar with— articles, books, images, documents, websites, and so on. Our students, however, live in a different digital universe than the one we most typically inhabit. They read comment fields on social networks such as Flickr or YouTube, where the insights one finds range from useful to ridiculous. They rely on content they find on Facebook. Blog posts are fair game for almost any use—unattributed facts or opinions become evidence to support factual claims without much critical reflection. Papers or projects posted online by students taking similar courses elsewhere are increasingly popular sources—of late, students have been asking me more and more often how to cite such papers in their own work. All too often, their first source of information is *Wikipedia.* Despite the well-intentioned, but almost surely failed, attempts of various history departments or individual faculty members to require their students to stay well away from all such "unreliable" sources, I think it is fair to say that students are probably largely unaffected by these prohibitions.[13] Moreover, it seems to me to be a professional conceit to say that unless historical content was created by or curated by professional scholars, it should not be used. Certainly our students tend to agree with this position.

Each of these four lessons that students have taught themselves about online historical content will be very familiar to anyone who has taught in the past decade. All point to some of the most significant problems we face as teachers trying to help our students develop sophisticated skills in our discipline. We already know that when students search for information, an Internet search engine is their default choice for locating information they seek, and that within the world of search engines, a significant majority of students use the one of the major ones such as Google, Yahoo, or Bing.[14] Only a small fraction of students begin their search elsewhere—a library catalog, a printed index, a research database, etc. Instead, they fire up their browser, type some likely key words into the search box, and begin scanning the results for something that seems useful. But not all the news is bad. For one thing, our students are very teachable. They want to know how to find the best resources they can to complete the work we are requiring of them, and only default to the most basic searching strategies when we have not taught them better ways to do their work. Moreover, as dependent as students are on web browsers to search for historical information, the good news is that these browsers increasingly link students to new sources of historical information—supermassive databases of images, such as Flickr; of genealogical data, such as Ancestry.com (which is not free); or videos, such as YouTube—as well as the legacy institutions such as the Library of Congress and National Archives. Even the external links on many *Wikipedia* entries often point students to useful resources for their research. These websites, all of which are "open archives"—meaning their content is not curated by professional archivists, but by the users themselves—offer students of history not only an even greater wealth of historical content, but also access to content created by those outside the small circle of professional scholars.

After all, students will do as they will, no matter what we say, and regardless of what one might think of open archive websites, major cultural players such as the Library of Congress and the National Archives have begun forays onto this playing field. As part of their participation in the Flickr Commons project, librarians at the Library of Congress analyzed what had happened to the images they had added from their collection to the Flickr database, and found that users of the website were interacting with Library of Congress content in a very active manner.[15] In October 2008, more than 4,600 images had been tagged slightly more than 67,000 times—of which 14,472 were judged to be "unique tags," that is, not duplicating a version of one already there—by 2,518 individual users. More than 2,500 individuals had added just over 7,000 comments to 2,873 images posted to the website by the library's staff.[16] The judgment of the authors of the library's report is that Flickr members substantially improved the metadata on the images and generally took their work seriously—that is, there were few off-color or inappropriate tags or comments on the images. As more and more of the "legacy institutions" such as the Library of Congress or the National Archives move their content into spaces where users can add tags and comments, it will become even more important for students to learn how to work with these add-ons to traditional historical content. For example, many in the older generation of historians (of which I am a charter member) were taught to use the Library of Congress subject headings as the quickest and best way to sort through any library's card catalog. In an era of keyword searching, the Library of Congress subject classifications are but one of many ways to dig around in databases, and so it is now already high time to teach history students about metadata—

what it is, how it works, how it governs searching, what the Dublin Core is, and so on.[17]

To date, historians have not been good about training students to use, find, and make use of historical content found online. In fact, some of the advice found in popular guides to success in history courses offer advice that borders on quaint in light of what we know about how students search for historical information when planning a research paper, or simply trying to prepare for tomorrow's class discussion. For instance, *Doing History: Research and Writing in the Digital Age* by Michael Galgano, J. Chris Arndt, and Raymond Hyser offers the following advice to history students as they begin a research project: "commence with a close review of a published guide. Currently, the standard is . . . *Reference Sources in History: An Introductory Guide.*" Students are then advised to consult printed bibliographies such as Robert Balay's *Guide to Reference Books*, or the *Bibliographic Index: A Cumulative Bibliography of Bibliographies.*[18] As worthy as this advice is, I think it is fair to say that very few of today's students are going to slog through a bibliography of bibliographies when Google and Yahoo are singing their song of immediate gratification. That siren song is both more attractive, and more comforting. As Steve Ramsey points out, "Google might seem something else entirely, but it shares the basic premise of those quaint guides of yore, and of all guides to knowledge. The point is not to return the over three million pages that relate in some way to Frank Zappa. The point is to say, 'Relax. Here is where you start. Look at this. Then look at that.'"[19] Moreover, because the Google interface is the one so many students use to find other things on the Internet, it is doubly comforting to use when they need a historical source, or three.

Other popular guides to success in the college history class are a bit more in tune with student research practices, but even these display a relatively restricted vision of what can and cannot be done online, limiting their advice to urging students to be cautious when using online sources, but offer little or no practical advice when it comes to assessing the reliability of information they find online. Moreover, because most prescriptive guides aimed at students urge their audience to stick to websites with .edu addresses, or that are associated with institutions such as major research libraries, museums, and archives, these guides all but shut out the possibility that quality historical content can be found elsewhere. For instance, a student who followed this advice about limited searching would miss out on worthy sites such as one offering an exhibition of the photography of Li Zhensheng (Red-ColorNewsSoldier.com), or a playful website offering up hundreds of primary sources from the life of Marshall Tito of Yugoslavia (Titoville.com).[20] Each of these .com websites provides visitors with very worthy historical resources, and so provides convincing proof of why students should not limit themselves to a small subset of the websites available to them. Moreover, the advice to stick to known, reliable websites is focused almost entirely on the Web 1.0 version of what online historical content was; that is, websites containing collections of historical sources. A student will be hard-pressed to find any advice on what to make of historical content found on blogs, open archives, social networking websites, video sharing websites, or Twitter. For instance, as part of its commemoration of the 150th anniversary of the Civil War, the *Washington Post* has decided to "Tweet the Civil War" with "commentary from experts, sesquicentennial news and an updating event calendar" on a special Twitter feed.[21] What is an enterprising history student to do with tweets like this one?

> **CivilWarwp To Lt Slemmer:** [Gen Scott] directs that u take measures 2 . . . prevent the seizure of the forts in Pensacola Harbor by surprise or assault. 9:50 PM Jan 3rd via HootSuite.[22]

Similarly, an enterprising student will certainly find no help in these prescriptive guides when it comes to deciding whether or not to use and if so, how to use, content such as Errol Morris's excellent blog series on Roger Fenton's faked photographs from the Crimean War (mentioned in the introduction).[23] Even a guide to world history online, which I wrote with my colleagues Kelly Schrum and Kristin Lehner, limits its discussion of online historical content to Web 1.0 websites.[24]

Given that students receive so little advice on how to find and assess historical content online, a brief case study seems to be in order. This case study deals with a conventional website, rather than one that is interactive. Teaching students to make effective use of (and create) historical content found in the new types of websites that have begun to appear in what we like to call the Web 2.0 world is dealt with in more detail in subsequent chapters.

A Case Study in Historical Searching

At the top of the pyramid of how students find historical content sits the search engine. What happens when a student doing a keyword search in

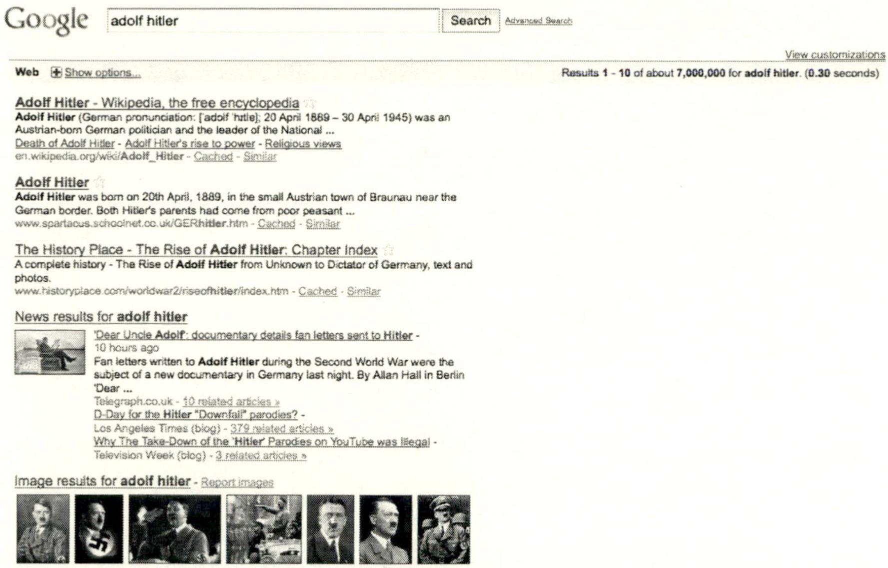

Fig. 2. Screenshot of the first page of Google search results for "Adolf Hitler" on April 26, 2010 (First Half).

a search engine finds themselves confronted with hundreds of thousands, or even millions, of possible search results? Or, what happens when the results that come up early in a search are of dubious quality? In the earlier example of our student who was looking for a few good sources about the Holocaust, what if, as part of his search, he had typed "Adolf Hitler" into his Google search box? On April 26, 2010, that search would have returned the result as shown in figure 2.

The second half of the screen shown in figure 3 includes a website—the Adolf Hitler Historical Museum—as one of the top results. Google is not alone in pushing the Hitler Historical Museum toward the top of its search returns. In addition to a Google search, a student doing research on Hitler might find this website as an external link on Wikimedia's page of Hitler quotations.[25] A Yahoo search on the delimited term "Adolf Hitler" places the Hitler Historical Museum third overall in the list of suggested websites, and the Yahoo directory search places it second. In fact, every other search engine (Bing, AltaVista, Dogpile, etc.) I tested in April 2010 returned the Hitler Historical Museum on the first page of search results. As a result, a

Image results for **adolf hitler** - Report images

The History Place - The Rise of Adolf Hitler: Chapter Index
A complete history - The Rise of **Adolf Hitler** from Unknown to Dictator of Germany, text and photos.
www.historyplace.com/worldwar2/riseofhitler/ - Cached - Similar

Adolf Hitler
A synopsis of key points about **Adolf Hitler** and his significance from an educational site on the Holocaust.
remember.org/guide/Facts.root.hitler.html - Cached - Similar

Adolf Hitler
The story of the Nazi Führer and his road to power.
www.**adolfhitler**.dk/ - Cached - Similar

Hitler Historical Museum
The Hitler Historical Museum is a non-biased, non-profit museum devoted to the study and preservation of the world history related to **Adolf Hitler** and the ...
www.**hitler**.org/ - Cached - Similar

Amazon.com: Adolf Hitler: The Definitive Biography (9780385420532 ...
Adolf Hitler, Soviet Union, Prime Minister, National Socialism, Red Army, United States .....
5.0 out of 5 stars **Adolf Hitler**, a superlative popular history ...
www.amazon.com › ... › People, AZ › (H) › Hitler, Adolf - Cached - Similar

Adolf Hitler (dictator of Germany) -- Britannica Online Encyclopedia
Britannica online encyclopedia article on **Adolf Hitler** (dictator of Germany), April 20, 1889Braunau am Inn, AustriaApril 30, 1945Berlin, Germanyleader of ...
www.britannica.com/EBchecked/topic/267992/**Adolf-Hitler** - Cached - Similar

Adolf Hitler Biography - Biography.com
Learn about the life of **Adolf Hitler** at Biography.com. Read Biographies, watch interviews and videos.
www.biography.com/articles/**Adolf-Hitler**-9340144 - Cached - Similar

Fig. 3. Screenshot of the first page of Google search results for "Adolf Hitler" on April 26, 2010 (Second Half).

student trying to do some web research on Adolf Hitler is all but doomed to find his or her way to this website.[26]

The practical experience of teachers and the findings of researchers indicate that a typical student is very likely to click on the museum website simply because it shows up on the first page of search results. This path of least resistance approach to searching—exemplified by the student in Lesson 1 (Google Makes College Easy)—would almost certainly take a student researcher to the website shown in figure 4.

The website helpfully offers that it "is a non-biased, non-profit museum devoted to the study and preservation of the world history [*sic*] related to Adolf Hitler and the National Socialist Party. True to its role as an educational museum, these exhibits allow for visitors to understand and examine

Hitler Historical Museum

"If freedom is short of weapons, we must compensate with willpower."
-- Adolf Hitler, Landsberg, 5 November 1925

Introduction

The Hitler Historical Museum is a non-biased, non-profit museum devoted to the study and preservation of the world history related to Adolf Hitler and the National Socialist Party. True to its role as an educational museum, these exhibits allow for visitors to understand and examine historical documents and information for themselves. The museum, while acknowledging the tragedy that over 50 million people died during World War 2, retains its non-biased status by refraining from making political judgments of any sort. Neither does it make the standard, uninformative, and cliched historical judgement that the victor of the war was "good" and that the loser of the war was "bad." Instead, all materials and resources are provided as a documentation of the time period and as scholastic resources with notes for clarification. No biased judgments, slanderous labels or childish name calling exist here as they do in most of the writings on this topic.

The Museum's chief concern is to provide documents and information that shed light on Adolf Hitler and the National Socialist Party. Because of the numerous contradicting, disjoint, biased, confused, and deficient interpretations that exist, few scholars are able to gather the facts and to understand and explain them coherently. Whether this failure is from a lack of information, scholarship ability, or honesty is unimportant. What is important is that historical information be made freely available and gathered into exhibits that allow researchers to derive indepedent conclusions from the relatively well preserved writings of this time period.

Fig. 4. Screenshot of the Adolf Hitler Historical Museum (http://www.hitler.org) on May 3, 2010.

historical documents and information for themselves." At some point in their education, most students have been taught that they should search for information from "non-biased" sources, such as this website claims to be, because then they can decide for themselves what the information means, free from any bias of the website's creator(s). To make sure that visitors to the site get this point, the website continues.

The Museum's chief concern is to provide documents and informa-tion that shed light on Adolf Hitler and the National Socialist Party. Because of the numerous contradicting, disjoint [sic], biased, confused, and deficient interpretations that exist, few scholars are able to gather the facts and to understand and explain them coherently. Whether this failure is from a lack of information, scholarship ability, or honesty is unimportant. What is important is that historical information be made freely available and gathered into exhibits that allow researchers to derive indepedent [sic] conclusions from the relatively well preserved writings of this time period.[27]

Despite the two typographical errors in this paragraph, I think it is safe to say that many students visiting the site would find this line of argument compelling. After all, the site must be good, because it appears on the first page of Google results, and it is simply offering facts (non-biased facts) in a way that will allow the user to draw his or her own conclusions. It is not just students who do not look carefully at websites before including them in their work. A search of college library websites turned up a number that provide their students with unannotated links to the website of the Hitler Historical Museum.[28] Similarly, Random House offers a similarly unannotated link to the website from their page promoting sales of a children's book on the Holocaust.[29] Even college faculty members provide their students with helpful links to this site.[30] And mainstream news media such as *Newsweek* (perhaps unwittingly) provide links to the site on their own website.[31] These various links compete with links to websites offering seemingly excellent term papers about Adolf Hitler for sale at attractive prices, and links to other neo-Nazi websites such as Stormfront.org (purveyors of the similarly problematic websites such as martinlutherking.org).

When I was a college freshman in the 1970s, one of my history professors took those of us in his course on European diplomatic history to the main university library to teach us how to use a research library—as opposed to our high school or local public library. He introduced us to cutting-edge information resources such as the *Reader's Guide to Periodical Literature,* gave us a brief primer on using Library of Congress subject headings in the card catalog—which stretched on as far as we could see—and took us into the stacks to show us how serendipity could also play a role in finding a good book to use for a paper. By the end of the hour, I was overloaded with information, but I also had acquired the most basic level of what we now call "information literacy," and so could begin to try to find what I needed in a more organized, and at least a slightly sophisticated way. What information literacy skills do we teach our students today that might help them avoid websites like the Hitler Historical Museum? The answer, unfortunately, is that most of us do not teach such skills. It could be that we make the mistake of assuming that because our students are adept users of technology, they are therefore adept learners with technology. Or it could be that we ourselves do not know much about how to drill down into websites to learn more about the website itself. If the problem is the former, then it is high time to stop assuming that students know what they are doing when they search for information online. If the problem is the latter, then the example of the Hitler Historical Museum will help demonstrate just what it is students need to know when they venture onto the Internet in search of historical content.

The Adolf Hitler Historical Museum

We have already seen that anyone searching for historical information about Adolf Hitler is being prompted by various search engines and by other resources to visit the Adolf Hitler Historical Museum.[32] We have also seen that the website claims to be an unbiased source for information about Hitler, and we have seen that the front page of the website includes some spelling and syntactical errors—an early clue that we ought to be suspicious of the content on the site. After all, if the creators of a website cannot be bothered to make sure their home page is free from such errors, can we trust them to make sure that the rest of the site is similarly free from errors—errors such as the proper citation of sources, and other similar things historians care about? What follows is a step-by-step approach to learning more about the Hitler Historical Museum's website. This same approach can be used with any website with varying degrees of success, depending on how transparent the website's creators/owners are, and whether organizations such as the Internet Archive have collected copies of older versions of the website.

Step 1—Who Owns the Website?

Whenever we assign a book, an article, or a primary source to students, one of the first things we ask them to take note of is who the author is. Sometimes that information is easily available, sometimes it is difficult or impossible to discern, but we always ask them to try to find the author and, if possible, to learn something about the author or creator. After all, if you know something about the author, you may gain some insight into what he or she has written or created. Students visiting websites should not be given a pass on finding out who the author/creator of the website (or a portion of the site) might be. The simplest way to find out something about who made a website is to look for a link to an "About" page. "About" pages vary in quality and in the amount of information they disclose about the author(s) of the website—ranging from a full-disclosure page, such as the one we created at the Center for History and New Media for the website Making the History of 1989—and the Hitler Historical Museum, which offers no such information to visitors.[33] When teaching my students how to work with websites, I tell them that the lack of an "About" page is often (but not always) a telling clue. Why would the website's creator(s) not take credit for the work they have done? The reason is not always sinister, but it could be that the site's creator(s) have deliberately chosen to keep their role in the site obscure. At a minimum, the lack of an "About" page should make one curious to know more.

But how can we find out more about a website's creators if they do not offer such information? Too often we assume that such information is not available when it often is. For instance, the website WhoIs.com offers users the opportunity to examine the registration information of many websites. Website owners can keep this information private in certain circumstances, but often they do not, either because they do not mind the world having access to such information, or simply because they do not realize that the registration information for their website is being published. In the case of the Hitler Historical Museum, a "WhoIs" search tells us that on April 26, 2010, the domain hitler.org was owned by an entity named "United . Thought." The domain was created on March 12, 1998, and the current registration will expire on March 11, 2017. United . Thought lists an address of 527 3rd Street, San Francisco, CA 94107, and a telephone number of 415-367-3800. The email contact information in the record is accounts@utindustries.com (fig. 5).

A simple web search on the information made available through WhoIs .com does not reveal very much. The website utindustries.com was not active on May 3, 2010, and a check of the telephone number in the Internet White Pages revealed only that the number is for an unpublished listing for a landline telephone in Sausalito, California. A quick check of Google Maps and using the Street View feature reveals a picture of the address, but no further information. The owner(s) of the domain occupy one of the residential units above the diner and coffee shop on the street level of this building. Beyond that, we cannot learn anything else about the owners from these simple search queries. But what if we dig a little deeper into the morass of information that is the Internet?

Fig. 5. Screenshot of Google Maps, with A marking 527 3rd Street, San Francisco, CA 94107.

A simple question to ask about the owner of any Internet domain is what other domains that person or organization also owns. Digging further into the domain registration and address data provided by the simple WhoIs search, we find that United . Thought had an earlier address in Herndon, Virginia—an address that turns out to be a postal box at a store in a strip mall. We also learn that this same organization owns several domains that are devoted to Nazism and current National Socialist politics, including siegheil.org and nazi.org. The latter website is the home of the Libertarian National Socialist Green Party (a neo-Nazi organization). This educated poking around online resulted in a picture of the Hitler Historical Museum as part of a network of websites devoted to current neo-Nazi politics in North America, and owned by a person or an organization in San Francisco. Finding out more about the site's owner would require, among other things, traveling to San Francisco or hiring a private investigator—both clearly beyond the pale of any basic information literacy lesson. But simply knowing the owner(s) of the Hitler.org website also own a series of neo-Nazi websites calls into question the website's claim to be unbiased in its presentation of information about Hitler and his career.

Step 2—What Metadata Does the Website Use to Attract Visitors?

Commercial websites pay a great deal of attention to what is known in the industry as "search engine optimization"—a term that means using tricks of the trade to maximize the likelihood that one's website will show up early in the results of a query typed into a search engine. Among the many strategies used to improve a website's position in the search rankings is to include various keywords in the metadata of the website's home or index page. Metadata—quite literally "data about data" —sits out of sight in the HTML code that describes the website, and can only be seen by viewing the website's source data through options available on various web browsers. Website creators include likely keywords in that metadata so that when search engines index their website, those keywords are picked up in the indexing process. When search engine users type in the same keywords, they are more likely to be routed directly to that page than if the metadata did not include those terms. For this reason, examining the metadata a website's creator(s) insert can offer useful clues to what sorts of search traffic they are trying to attract. The Hitler Historical Museum home page includes the following metadata:

> <meta name="description" content="The Hitler Historical Museum is a non-biased, non-profit museum devoted to the study and preservation of the world history related to Adolf Hitler and the National Socialist Party.">

> <meta name="keywords" content="Hitler, Adolf, Adolf Hitler, National Socialism, Nazi, Nazis, History, World War Two, Jews, Jewry, Jewish, Hindenburg">

What do we learn from these metadata? The "description" is what shows up in a search engine under the link to the website. From the keywords used on this website we can see what the website's creator(s) believed were the terms most likely to animate a search for content on their website. Search companies such as Google and Yahoo keep the specifics of their algorithms secret, but the degree to which a website rises or falls in the results from a keyword search is a function of a variety of factors—including how often the website is linked to from other websites, the keywords in the metadata, the appearance of keywords on individual web pages, and the frequency of the appearance of those keywords—just to name a few of the important factors. A quick test of the Hitler Museum's website using each of the keywords in the site's metadata demonstrates that keywords alone are not enough to push a site up in the search returns. While the terms "Hitler," "Adolf," "Adolf Hitler" all showed up on the first page of a Google search on May 4, 2010, other terms such as "National Socialism" did not bring up the museum's website until the twenty-fifth page of the search results, and the rest required even more scrolling through results. It is probably safe to say that the average student is not going to keep searching beyond the first few pages of search results.

Step 3—What Is the History of the Website?

As historians, we believe that the history of a thing, an event, or a person is worthy of careful study. Fortunately, the history of most websites can now be studied in much the same way that we study other things. There is even an archive where we can conduct our research—the Internet Ar-

Hitler Historical Museum

Adolf Hitler, born 20 April 1889

"If freedom is short of weapons, we must compensate with willpower."
-- Adolf Hitler, Landsberg, 5 November 1925

Introduction

The Hitler Historical Museum is a non-biased, non-profit museum devoted to the study and preservation of the world history related to Adolf Hitler and the National Socialist Party. True to its role as an educational museum, these exhibits allow for visitors to understand and examine historical documents and information for themselves. The museum, while acknowledging the tragedy that over 50 million people died during World War 2, retains its non-biased status by refraining from making political judgements of any sort. Neither does it make the standard, uninformative, and cliched historical judgement that the victor of the war was "good" and that the loser of the war was "bad." Instead, all materials and resources are provided as a documentation of the time period and as scholastic resources with notes for clarification. No biased judgements,

Fig. 6. Screenshot of an earlier version of the Adolf Hitler Historical Museum, April 20, 2011. Courtesy of the Internet Archive.

chive (archive.org).[34] The Internet Archive offers users access to billions of web pages, most of which are archived copies of websites collected by web crawlers since 1996. In the case of the Hitler Historical Museum, 692 versions of the website were collected and archived between December 5, 1998, and May 3, 2010.[35] The original version of the Hitler Historical Museum's website is not so helpful in our historical investigation, largely because it doesn't say much more than what the current version of the website tells us. But historians know that thorough historical research means looking at all of the available evidence, not merely the first and last versions of an artifact like a website.

The original Internet Archive (IA) interface made it easy for users to decide which of the 692 website captures to view, because there was an asterisk next to each new version of the site the IA web crawler found. Thus, the version of the site found on April 20, 2001 (fig. 6), offers clear evidence to even the most skeptical visitor that this website—despite its claims to being "non-biased," is actually a pro-Nazi website.[36] Any website offering up a birthday cake and birthday greetings for one of the world's worst dictators is probably not quite as unbiased as it might claim to be. Unfortunately, the current version (in late 2011) of the Internet Archive's display of its web captures no longer includes the update asterisks, so users must now click through the various versions of a site held in the archive to find changes or updates. Nevertheless, the archive remains a powerful tool for locating and analyzing website content from the past.

Step 4—Search for the Reviews of the Website

When we select a book that we might use in our own scholarly work, one of the first things we do is check the various historical journals to see if any reviews of the book have been written. At this writing, there were no scholarly reviews of the Hitler Museum website that could be located either online or in my university's library. Despite the lack of scholarly reviews of this particular website, there are often reviews available for websites containing historical content, whether through organizations such as the Roy Rosenzweig Center for History and New Media (where I work); or in historical journals; on the websites of historical organizations; or in the blogs written by historians, both in and outside of academia. Students should always be encouraged to seek out such reviews if they intend to use material from a website, just in case they find themselves at a location like Hitler.org.

It is worth noting here that it is not only students who use information found online in uncritical ways. For instance, the recently published book *Hitler's Engineers: Fritz Todt and Albert Speer—Master Builders of the Third Reich* by Blaine Taylor (Casemate Publishers, 2010) cites the Hitler Historical Museum as an authoritative source on page 56. Even more egregious is the case of the publisher of a recent fourth grade history textbook approved for adoption by the Virginia State Board of Education, which makes the false claim that thousands of slaves fought willingly on the side of the Confederacy during the Civil War. When pressed to explain where she found evidence for this howler, the author, Joy Masoff, explained that she found this information through online searches.[37] If professional authors and editors cannot be bothered to check the veracity of evidence they find online, it is no surprise that students are also loath to do so. It is unlikely that they will go to all the trouble I have laid out above with my case study of Hitler.org, but exposing them to these steps is akin to the tour of the university library my professor gave me so long ago. If they know how to work with websites, they can do so when the need arises. When I walk my own students through the Hitler Historical Museum exercise, their eyes are opened not only to the need for more careful thinking about the websites they use in their research, but also to the need to better understand the ways historians can investigate the background of the sources they find online. After this exercise, I find that they are much more careful consumers of online historical content.

Teaching our students how to search is as important today as it was forty years ago when searching meant making sense of the card catalog in a library, or finding aids in an archive. Students have access to so many more information resources that it can be bewildering to think about the many ways they access that information. One important reason why students often turn to the information resources they already know is that the important legacy institutions often make it quite difficult to find what you want on their websites. The typical web user has grown accustomed to the spare search page of Google, or the slightly busier interface of Yahoo, or one of the other search engines. For all of their problems discussed earlier, the search companies have mastered the art of the clean delivery of information to searchers. At the other end of the spectrum are the big institutions such as the Library of Congress, the National Archives, or the British Museum. These institutions built their search interfaces a long time ago in Internet years, and for a variety of reasons—some good, some not so good—have stuck with their existing systems for finding information. Students used to the clean lines of the search engine pages and the simple system of typing in some likely keywords often throw up their hands in despair when confronted by the more complex systems of the legacy institutions. Thus, if we want them to use these resources, rather than relying on basic searches with search engines, or on social networks, we have to teach them how to slog their way through these difficult and often bewildering interfaces.

For example, one of the largest repositories of online historical primary sources—the American Memory project of the Library of Congress—first takes a visitor to a browse page that offers the opportunity to browse the collection by topic from a list selected by the librarians, or if one looks carefully in the upper right-hand corner of the screen, a search box is also available for those likely keywords students have come to love. If one were looking for a map of the Chesapeake Bay in the late nineteenth century, here is what would happen. Click on the "maps" link and a new browse page appears, offering the opportunity to search across eleven different collections: everything from Civil War maps, to maps of the national parks, to maps of Liberia. A search across all of the eleven collections on the keywords "Chesapeake Bay" turns up thirty-nine images of maps, which can be seen in thumbnail form if one notices the small option for "Gallery View." If thirty-nine maps seems like too many, given that we are only interested in the nineteenth century, selecting only the "Maps and Cartographic items" collection yields the same thirty-nine maps. If, however, you persist and click on the link that says "Map Collections," you will be taken to another page altogether that gives you the chance to search the library's map collections in a different (and even older) way. If one clicks on the Geographic Location Index, what one finds is a list of Library of Congress subject headings by geographic location. A Chesapeake Bay map might reasonably be found in either Virginia or Maryland. And sure enough, there is a subject heading called "United States—Maryland—Chesapeake Bay." Clicking on this link yields six maps, none from the late nineteenth century. What about Virginia? There are two Library of Congress subject headings for Virginia and the Chesapeake Bay: "United States—Virginia—Chesapeake Bay" and "United States—Virginia—Chesapeake Bay Region." Clicking on the first of these offers up five of the six maps you found by trying the Maryland links. Clicking on the second produces the missing sixth map. Can you imagine a typical student persisting any further in his or her search of the Library of Congress website? Probably not. Unless, that is, we teach our typical student easier ways into the databases of the large institutions like the Library of Congress and show him or her just how rich those information resources are.

For example, a Google search proves to be more helpful in a roundabout way. Searching on "historical maps of Virginia" turns up some interesting options on the first search return page, including a link to the Library of Virginia (http://lva.virginia.gov), which has a reasonably significant number of maps posted online. A visit to the Digital Collections portions of their website, and from there to the Alan M. Voorhees Map Collection, turns up some possible candidates for a student's research project. Probably the best—despite the fact that it is dated 1849, and therefore is outside the desired time frame—is "A new map of Maryland and Delaware: with their canals, roads & distances."[38] This map, available as a ten-megabyte download, provides a great deal of detail on the Maryland and Virginia portions of the upper bay—that is, everything north of Tangier Island—and was much easier to locate than maps in the American Memory Project files. The search facility on the Library of Virginia's website is much more intuitive than the one on the Library of Congress's site, and is not at all dependent on students knowing how to work with Library of Congress subject headings.

By contrast, if our student had been searching for a copy of Lincoln's Gettysburg Address in his own handwriting, a simple search at the American Memory Project website would have turned up several excellent options on the first keyword search. Similarly, a search on "George Washington, March 15, 1783," would quickly and easily turn up images of General Washington's speech at Newburgh, New York, that effectively ended a brewing rebellion of Continental Army officers. The lesson here is that the more famous and/or heavily used a document is, the more easily it is found in systems like the one at the Library of Congress. Because students are often searching for historical sources that are more obscure, it is incumbent on us to teach our students (a) how to work with multiple finding tools, and (b) how to get beyond any frustration they might have with search engines that are not as seemingly simple as Google or Yahoo. Just as my history professors could not and did not assume that I knew how to work in a university research library, we must make the same assumptions of our students. They need concrete examples of how to find and analyze content they find online—especially more obscure content that would not show up on the first few pages of a Google search. Prescriptive advice to "be careful about what you find online" teaches them nothing, and is counterproductive at best.

In addition to using search engines or the websites of the large cultural institutions to search for historical content, students can—and do—

approach the task of finding historical information in a variety of ways. One that is becoming increasingly common might be called "social searching." Because social networks such as Facebook are so important in students' lives, it should be no surprise that they often turn to these networks for help in finding information they need to complete assignments. Imagine for a moment you are a university student sitting in the student union, your apartment, the local coffee shop, or wherever you get a wireless signal, and you need to come up with some information for a history paper due two days from now. You have put off the thing for a while, but now you really need to get started. Sure, your professor suggested some good possible sources for the paper, but this is, after all, the age of just-in-time delivery of everything from flowers, to books, to information. So you stare at your screen for inspiration and see several windows open—Facebook, iTunes, YouTube, and several small IM conversation windows. What to do? What to do? Imagine further that your paper is for a class on the civil rights movement. A quick Google search turns up just over 73 million hits, so you enclose your search in quotation marks—a nifty move that cuts down on the number of possible websites to just over 164,000. That will not do, will it? Hmm. Facebook? A search of Facebook turns up the "community page" for the civil rights movement.

But only nineteen people "like" this page—not much of a community— and the only information on the page is the *Wikipedia* entry that came up first in your Google search. But at least there are some faces you remember from slides your professor showed in class—Martin Luther King Jr., Rosa Parks, Malcolm X, and W.E.B. DuBois. Maybe they have their own community pages—and sure enough, they do. The community page for Martin Luther King Jr. has almost 3,000 fans, and the "Global Related Posts" being fed onto the page by the Facebook information engine includes several quotations that might just be the starting point for a paper.[39]

"The time is always right to do what is right."

"Everything that is done in the world is done by hope."

If you are lucky, you choose the first quotation, because it is indeed by Martin Luther King Jr., and your paper focuses on King's ideas of timely action in the face of opposition. If you are unlucky, you choose the second, because even though it seems like a nice echo of the 2008 campaign slogan of President Barack Obama, it is not a quotation from Martin Luther

"Everything that is done in the world is done by hope."

Fig. 7. Photograph, by the author, of a misattributed button offered for sale at http://www.toppun.com/Martin-Luther-King/Buttons/Everything-that-is-done-in the-world-is-done-by-hope-Martin-Luther-King-Jr-BUTTON.html.

King, but rather from the Reverend Martin Luther. Even though you can buy a Martin Luther King Jr. button with this quotation on it (fig. 7), the original comes from the sixteenth-century German theologian, and has been misattributed to the civil rights campaigner for a long time—especially online (or at least so it says in Wikiquotes under "MLK").[40]

What about a search of YouTube? A quick search on Martin Luther King Jr. turns up the full broadcast of King's famous "I Have a Dream" speech as the first hit, the last minute of his final speech in Memphis as the second, and in fourth position, an edited version of the CBS News broadcast in which Walter Cronkite announces King's death.[41] Watching these videos, viewed by others a total of over 11,500,000 times in May 2010, gives you that final kick in the pants you need to get moving on the paper—after all, King's quotation about the timing being right echoes in your ear and off you go.

This brief example demonstrates that students can use social media such as Facebook for historical research for good or ill. If, as our student, you chose the first example, you would have found inspiration for your paper—an organizing principle around which the rest of your research could revolve—from what random people around the world posted on their Facebook pages about Martin Luther King Jr. You could gain further inspiration from the historical videos you watch, and perhaps think up some other promising avenues of research. If, however, you chose the second quotation, you might have found yourself in hot water with your professor if he or she knew that this particular quotation was a misattribution. Is it better or worse for our student to begin searching for information on the civil rights movement on Facebook—where he or she is led to one web page—or in Google, where tens of thousands of possible results pop up on the computer screen? The answer, of course, is both and neither at the same time. Instead of railing against students' use of social media, we need to meet them where they live and teach them—just as in the example of the Hitler Historical Museum—how to make the most of and avoid the pitfalls of these sorts of information resources. For example, given their powerful dependence on *Wikipedia* as a go-to source about the past, a productive fifteen minutes can be spent in any history class showing students the "history" tab on any *Wikipedia* entry and how, if one scrolls back through earlier versions of an entry, it is possible to chart the ebb and flow of that entry's content over time. In my own experience, this brief exercise is often an eye-opener for most of my students who are used to looking at *Wikipedia* as simply another online encyclopedia, not as a living archive of public debate over how information in that encyclopedia ought to be presented to the public. Once they understand that the history of a *Wikipedia* entry is both accessible and has something to teach us about the construction of knowledge in public space through the use of social media, their go-to source suddenly becomes much more interesting as a historical resource.

For all of the ways that social media such as Facebook, YouTube, and *Wikipedia* capture students' attention while linking them to one another in new and interesting ways, the use of a computer to find and analyze historical content remains a potentially isolating practice. Confronted with a class assignment, too often students sit down at their computer, work their way through various searching and analytical strategies, and do the best they can on their own. They might send an instant message or a text message to a friend seeking help, or they might post a plea for assistance on Facebook, but more often than not, they simply try to tough it out on their own without recourse to the sorts of collaborative opportunities the technology now provides. To address this issue, I have designed a number of assignments over the years that force students together around the finding and analysis of online sources. One of the most successful of these falls into the category of "online scavenger hunts," in which I give the students meeting in a computer lab a selection of ten images from the past and tell them that as soon as they can tell me what each image is and how it relates to our course, they receive their grade for the day and can leave. All of the images are downloaded from the Internet and each has been renamed so that the file name is not searchable. The first few are always easy for the students to identify, but as they work their way down the list, the images become more and more difficult to identify. At first, they try to complete the assignment on their own. As the minutes pass, the students begin to talk to one another about what they are or are not finding. By the time they get to the last two images (both of which are quite difficult to puzzle out) most, if not all, of the students have gotten up from their seats and they are clustered around one computer offering suggestions and discussing search strategies. When they finally puzzle out the last item, I make them all stop and point out that as the assignment became more difficult, they began to rely on one another more and more. Then I point out that historians do the same thing when we are doing our own work—we rely on the help of archivists, librarians, and colleagues to help us puzzle out the most difficult sources we find. The lesson I drive home in this exercise is that they should not allow the computer to isolate them from one another, and that by collaborating they get their work done more rapidly, and at a higher level of quality.

Digital media also make it possible now for our students to build complex and very user-friendly databases of references to the sources they find in their searching online and in the analog world. Reference management software packages, some of which now run as part of a student's web browser, make it possible for students not only to quickly and easily build databases of their sources, but also to annotate those sources, mark them up with keywords of their own devising, and share these sources with others, either as part of a group working on a particular project, or to simply share them with the entire world. Among the most popular of the reference management packages are Zotero (developed by the Center for History and New Media), Mendeley, and Connotea.[42] In the pre-digital age, students collected their resources for a history project—likely on three-by-five cards, or in a notebook—they would then would write their paper or complete the project in some other form, and then would either file those sources away, or throw them away as no longer useful. Even if they filed their sources away, accessing them again for a new project proved difficult. In the digital world, students using these reference management packages can now keep the results of their research in an easily accessible database that, if it is web based, they can access from anywhere at any time, and that they can continue to improve and add to throughout their academic careers. However, as user-friendly as these packages are, there is a learning curve that still requires history instructors to teach their students both how to use the packages and what the value of using such tools over time can be. In my experience, once students crest this not-very-steep curve, they wonder how it is they made it through school up to that point without using a reference manager of some sort.

A more recent problem that students (and we) face when it comes to using search engines to help us locate historical information is a shift by the major search companies, led by Google, toward personalized search results.[43] No longer are the results of a search the same for all users everywhere. Instead, since late 2009, Google has changed the process by which it returns information to a user, customizing those results based upon a whole series of factors, including the user's location and prior search history. What this means is that two students in the same class at the same university may well get wildly different search results from the same query, or that the same student (if he or she is not logged into the search engine's service when searching) may get two different sets of results, if one search is conducted in her apartment and the other from a computer on campus. I think it is fair to say, based upon my informal polling of my students, that they have no idea that their searching is being "managed" for them in this way by the search engine companies. In particular, they are surprised to find that significant amounts of historical information that they might find useful never makes its way to their desktop because whatever social search algorithm the company is using deems that information irrelevant to them.[44] A simple way to drive this lesson home is to have all students in a course execute the same search at approximately the same time, from wherever they happen to be at that moment, and then compare their results when they return to class. Invariably they find that their favorite search engines return different information and must then try to understand how to find the things they want rather than the things that the search company thinks they want.

Exercises such as the group scavenger hunt make it much easier to emphasize a final piece of advice that I give my students over, and over, and over—namely, that the best way to begin their historical research is to go to the campus library and chat with a librarian—preferably the liaison librarian for the history department. Over the years I have found that this particular piece of advice has to be repeated several times before it finally takes. After all, if you can call up ten million possible sources on Abraham Lincoln, who needs to talk to anyone? However, it is the overwhelming nature of that abundance of resources that often convinces my students that such a chat might actually be helpful. I point out to them that where once upon a time librarians were known as librarians, these days they are much better known as information specialists. Because they are trained not only to find useful information, but also how to teach others to find that information, a half hour spent with a librarian is often the difference between an "A" or a "B" on an assignment. Do they follow my advice? Only rarely. But the ones who do then come back to class and report to others that they saved themselves a tremendous amount of time and effort just by meeting with someone in the library. This particular insight is one that is not new in the digital age we live in. When I first started teaching at the college level, the Internet was in its infancy and so the help librarians gave in those days was focused largely on the card catalog and printed indices. Today, their skills as information specialists are even more important to our students. But whether students choose to visit the library or not, it remains essential for historians to teach them how to find the information they need, which means we need to engage much more actively with the methods our students use to find such information. If we do not, we are leaving it to them to puzzle out just what to do with ten million sources.

< 3 >

Analyzing

Making Sense of a Million Sources

When we think about the future of historical research in the age of the huge digital libraries that are currently under construction, we will face with what I sometimes think of as the Klofáč-Kramář dilemma.[1] In the late nineteenth and early twentieth centuries, Václav Klofáč and Karel Kramář were prominent Czech politicians—first in the Austro-Hungarian Empire, and later in Czechoslovakia.[2] Because neither man became president or had much of a reputation outside of parochial Czech political circles, you should not feel guilty if you have never heard of either one. But for historians of modern Czech politics (like me), they are central figures in the historical narrative of the first Czechoslovak republic. Kramář is fairly easy to research using conventional methods. The Kramář collection at the Archive of the National Museum (*Archiv Národního muzea*) in Prague contains more than one hundred boxes of manuscript sources from his life and career, and several other major archives in Prague, Brno, and Vienna contain significant numbers of primary sources devoted to Kramář. These primary sources are not (yet) digitized, and so one must journey to central Europe to see them, but they are reasonably well organized and readily available to researchers. There are several biographies of Kramář, at least a couple of which have real scholarly merit, and at last count scholars have published dozens of articles on Kramář. Historians know how to work with a subject such as Kramář and how to train our students how to work in archival collections like those devoted to his life.

We also know how to deal with a subject like Klofáč, even though he is much more difficult to pin down in the archives. Like Kramář, Klofáč has been the subject of several biographies; numerous (though fewer) scholarly articles; and, like his competitor for the attentions of Czech voters, he shows up regularly in histories of Czech politics from the 1880s to the beginning of the Second World War. However, researching Klofáč is a more difficult archival problem. Unlike Kramář, there is no major collection of Klofáč documents for the simple reason that when the Germans took full control of Czechoslovakia in the spring of 1939, Klofáč burned the vast majority of his personal archive, and after the Communist takeover of Czechoslovakia, his son destroyed the rest (his father having died during the war). The intent of these destructive acts was to keep these documents—many of which might have been used to implicate friends and colleagues—out of the hands of agents of repressive regimes. Thus, there are no shelves groaning under the weight of hundreds of boxes of Klofáč sources. But this lack of available sources does not mean Klofáč is invisible to historians—just more difficult to come to grips with. Researching Klofáč is much more of a scavenger hunt with many more miles of travel involved, but he lives in the collections of many dispersed archives around central Europe in letters he mailed to others, in articles he wrote for newspapers, in the minutes of meetings of the political party that he led for two decades, and in the reports of Austrian government spies who tracked him from his appearance on the political stage until his arrest for treason in 1914. Then there are the extensive transcripts of his trial for treason which include a lot of detailed testimony about his life and political activities. The "Klofáč archive" that is dispersed across all these repositories has also not been digitized, but almost certainly will be one day, along with the more easily accessed Kramář materials.

When that happens, as it almost surely will, given that these two men were founding fathers of the modern Czech state, what will historians do with those thousands and possibly tens of thousands of primary sources? At one level, access to and use of the Kramář archive will only be opened up and sped up. Instead of traveling to Prague, one will be able to work with the Kramář materials at a distance, and will be able to search through that archive with more speed and efficiency. By contrast, access to the Klofáč archive will be opened and sped up, but also historians will be able to create something like a unified collection through the aggregation of sources from those now scattered across central Europe. At this basic level, use of material from the lives of both Klofáč and Kramář will be easier for historians. What will be different is that if these materials are all marked up properly when they are digitized, it will be possible for historians to do much more than access these materials faster and from the comforts of home. We will also be able to start triangulating across a wide range of archival repositories that we had not previously thought of. So, for instance, was Kramář or Klofáč mentioned in a document in a collection we did not know existed? And if so, why and in what context? Similarly, we could chart the ebb and flow of a public figure's level of activity and/or interest value (to the public, to the secret police, in the media) by tracking how often he or she shows up in the sources.

Already, data-mining software makes it possible to link sources on the basis of date, location, names, institutional affiliations, and all the other ways historians triangulate between and among sources. In the past we have had to do that triangulation by hand, and so making these connections is often a laborious and imperfect process. With each passing week, more and more historical data appears online marked up in ways that make it possible for us to use new software tools to work with these data. Now software can make connections for us and possibly even propose new ways of thinking about things such as relationships between individuals.[3] As Greg Crane pointed out several years ago, "Already the books in a digital library are beginning to read one another and to confer among themselves before creating a new synthetic document for review by their human readers."[4] While Crane was writing about books "reading" one another, the same can already be said for non-book sources as well. The resulting "recombinant documents," as Crane calls them, offer the historian very different ways to look at and think about historical sources. Do we know what to do with such recombinant documents? And do we know how to train students how to work with such an overwhelming corpus of sources?

The answer, I propose, is both yes and no at the same time.

The "yes" part of the answer is that today's historians are well versed in thinking critically about historical sources, and those skills are not made obsolete by recombinant sources or by historical information presented to us in other ways such as can be done with sophisticated visualization software. But as useful as our current skills are, they are predicated on the form of the primary source. As Sam Wineburg has already demonstrated in his research on how historians think, historians approach primary sources in certain discipline-specific ways. Watch any historian read a letter written 100 years ago and you will see her or him check first for contextual data such as the date the letter was written, the author's name, the recipient's name, the place the letter was written, where it was mailed from and to, and any other data such as an institutional letterhead on the paper that might be available. Only when all of these bits of information have been mined from the source will the expert learner/historian begin reading the body of the letter. Novice learners, by contrast, tend to launch right into an examination of the main body of the source, coming back to contextual data only later, if at all.[5] Our goal in teaching historical methods is to train students to learn the same skills we have developed over many years of study and, we hope, to turn that learning into reading and analytical strategies that are as reflexive as ours are.

For example, although a personal letter increasingly seems like an artifact from a bygone era to students, they still know what a letter is, and so they apply whatever skills they have learned, just as we do, to the source in its original form. As any history teacher knows, students typically want the analysis of a personal letter to be relatively simple and straightforward. They want to know who the letter was from, whom it was addressed to, why it was written, and what it says. If some of the content is inflammatory or salacious, they (and we) naturally gravitate to that aspect of the letter. But if the letter seems pretty mundane on a first reading, they may quickly decide, "not much to learn here" and move on to the next source. Teaching them to read more carefully, to mine useful information from the seemingly mundane, is more difficult. Digital media make it possible to construct simple exercises that introduce students to the idea that something as seemingly simple and straightforward as a letter or a short telegram can be quite complex when read carefully.

Several years ago, back in the Web 1.0 era, my colleague Kelly Schrum and I designed a series of what at the time seemed like very interactive online exercises for students to introduce them to the complexities of working with historical documents such as personal letters, newspapers, maps, and so on. For the exercise on reading personal letters I selected a brief letter sent from Prague in the spring of 1939, just after the German takeover of the rump Czech state that had survived the Munich Conference disaster. This letter, sent from an American student to his cousin back in the United States, merrily recounts his bicycle ride across the Czech-German border, through the hills of northern Bohemia, and into Prague. Once in Prague he was witness to the German troops and tanks riding into town, and the inauguration of the Nazi Protectorate government. The letter is chatty, and the author breezily recounts the difficulties of his travel, some caused by the German takeover, some caused by the steep hills. I have assigned this letter to my students many times and only rarely do they extract any worthwhile insights from the text on the first reading. In our online exercise, my colleague and I posted up two versions of the letter—one without commentary, then a second with commentary from a historian (me). As the user drags his or her cursor over the text, the historian's commentary appears. For example, in the second paragraph, the author writes: "At first the Czechs got sore, blocked the streets, shook their fists at the troops, sang their national anthem, but when they saw more and more German troops pouring in, they saw their cause was hopeless and went back to their work." The text from the historian that pops up offers this commentary: "Historians are very interested in the supposed lack of resistance to the Nazis by Czech citizens. Kistler's account provides some verification of the common view that most Czechs simply did not resist. This is not news to specialists, but does provide further validation of one version of what happened in Prague."[6] This simple use of technology to give students a glimpse of more analytical reading strategies often prompts them to be much more analytical with later sources I give them. For example, when I next give them a personal letter to read and analyze, they are much more likely to think carefully about the historical context within which the letter was produced, asking themselves questions such as how the events swirling around the author might have (or might not have) colored his perceptions of what he was seeing, and why.

We are, as Greg Crane points out, on the cusp of an entirely more complex set of possibilities when it comes to using digital media to create teaching and learning opportunities for students than the one just described. For more than a decade, advocates of hypertext have promoted its value as a catalyst of new forms of reading. But hypertext built in HTML is inherently limited in its ability to create new forms of historical presentation, because HTML is a presentation language that describes what something will look like online (and what it is connected to elsewhere on the Internet). By contrast, XML describes the content it is marking up. A simple example can demonstrate the difference between the two languages. If one were to create a page of famous speeches by American presidents, the beginning of the source code for the page might look like the code below.

```
<html>
<head><title>Presidential Speeches</title></head>
<body>
<h2>Presidential Speeches</h2>
<hr>

<em>Farewell Address</em>, <b>George Washington</b>, 1796<br>
<em>Gettysburg Address</em>, <b>Abraham Lincoln</b>, 1863<br>
<em>Declaration of War</em>, <b>Franklin D. Roosevelt</b>,
1941<br>>

</body>
</html>
```

But in XML, the coding of that same content might look like the following.

```
<speeches>
<speech>
    <title>Farewell Address</title>
    <author>George Washington</author>
    <year>1796</year>
</speech>    .

<speech>
    <title>Gettysburg Address</title>
    <author>Abraham Lincoln</author>
    <year>1863</year>
</speech>

<speech>
    <title>Declaration of War</title>
    <author>Franklin D. Roosevelt</author>
    <year>1941</year>
</speech>
</speeches>
```

In the HTML code, the titles of the speeches are rendered in italics, while the names of the presidents are rendered in bold face type. In the XML code, none of this formatting exists, because such formatting decisions can be made by the user elsewhere, using cascading style sheets or other forms of formatting that, for instance, might define all titles of speeches as rendering in bold face, while the authors' names appear in italics. However, much more useful than formatting of text is the ability of users to extract information from historical documents marked up in XML by such fields as author, title, or year. In other words, in XML, the content and the form that content appears in are two separate things. XML makes recombinant documents possible.

To be sure, users of hypertextual documents—whether created in HTML or XML—do read in different ways than those whose documents contain no links. Whenever we click on a link we bounce from one source to another, sometimes returning to the original, sometimes not, but the various sources we see on-screen retain their shape and form—it is just how we get there and away from there that changes. But what happens when, instead of jumping from one document to another along hypertext links, our screen displays a recombinant document that has been parsed in ways that show only its references to a particular event—say a meeting of the party leadership to decide whether or not to form an electoral alliance with a rival party—and is simply part of a list of such references along with chunks of text that are devoted to that meeting? In other words, on-screen one might find the sentence from a letter written by a party leader dismissing the meeting as worthless, a three-sentence assessment of the meeting written by another participant who did not attend, but heard about it from someone else, and a half dozen other bits and pieces drawn from the archives of other politicians (and perhaps also government spies). Also on-screen might be a map showing not only the location of the meeting, but also the locations where each letter originated and/or was delivered, a time line showing the time sequence for each letter, and a link to the minutes of the meeting from the party's archive. What happens to the reflexive skill we have developed for reading letters when the letter is no longer a letter, but has been reduced to chunks and bits of a recombinant document?

This description of what one might find on-screen is not a fantasy of the future—it is already doable. The only impediment to the display of such recombinant documents is the marking up of the relevant documents, the writing of algorithms to scrape the relevant information from those documents, and a user interface that displays the scraped information in a way that is easy to read and work with. Such scraping algorithms already exist. Perhaps the most popular is the search engine Google. Think for a minute about what you see after typing some keywords into the Google search bar. The screen shows a combination of highlighted text, a snippet of information from the web resource (document, website, discussion forum posting, etc.), and some other relevant metadata including the current URL of the resource. Google also gives you the option of viewing your search results on a time line, or in other ways such as the Wonder Wheel. Now, instead of the search results you see from a Google search, imagine that you are working on a research project on the history of slavery in America and you decide to search through the personal correspondence of Thomas Jefferson for references to slaves and slavery. Instead of looking at search returns that take you to each individual letter Jefferson wrote in which he mentions slaves or slavery, you get a document that provides you with the paragraphs from those letters where slaves or slavery are discussed along with relevant contextual data such as dates, locations, recipient information, and so on. These paragraphs could be arranged in a variety of ways—chronologically, as part of a series of back and forth exchanges with individuals, or any other way you might choose. They would include a link back to the full document so that you could read the full text of whichever letter you chose, and you could view the sources either along a time line, on a map, or just as chunks of text on-screen. Already Google's book search makes a very limited version of such a recombinant document possible. Using Google Book Search you can search through a book for chunks of text that contain a word or phrase. A search on "slaves" in the 1829 text of Jefferson's *Notes on Virginia* turns up fifteen pages where the word "slaves" appears. What Google Book Search will not do is allow you to search across multiple texts simultaneously. Once librarians, archivists, historians, and the general public have completed the task of marking up corpuses of text like Jefferson's correspondence, it will be relatively easy to produce recombinant sources that work as described earlier.[7] This is the world we need to train our students for, but first we ourselves need to learn how to make use of these tools, and we need to be part of the discussion of how they are implemented in our field.[8]

More historical texts than can easily be counted have already been scanned and placed online: Google has scanned more than 20 million books, and is scanning new works at the rate of 1,000 pages per hour; other smaller projects such as the Open Content Alliance, the Million Books Project, and others are likewise making millions of books available online;

digital repositories of scholarly articles are also growing at a rate almost unimaginable just a few years ago.[9] For example, as of May 11, 2010, the JS-TOR database contained 37,307,998 pages from 6,219,336 articles in 1,239 journals.[10] LexisNexis claims to offer access to "billions of searchable documents and records."[11] The number of digitized primary sources is growing at a similarly rapid rate. The Europeana.eu project aggregates more than 20 million digitized primary sources.[12] The American Memory Project at the Library of Congress now offers more than 15 million primary sources in digital form, and just one newspaper scanning project—ProQuest Historical Newspapers—offers access to more than 25 million digitized pages.[13] These numbers do not even take into account the amount of digital data we are producing every year that future historians will have to grapple with—perhaps as many as 1,200 exabytes in 2010 with growth rates as high as 60 percent per year predicted through 2014.[14] One can only hazard a guess at how many historical primary sources will be available in digital form a decade from now when today's undergraduate students will be writing their dissertations, teaching high school history classes, creating museum exhibits, or building their own digital exhibitions just for fun.

Recombinant sources such as those described earlier are just one way that historians and history students are and will be working with digitized sources in the coming decade. As of this writing, there are not enough historical sources marked up in XML format nor are the analytical algorithms up to the tasks we would like to set for them, but it is only a matter of time—probably just a few years—before Crane's vision can be realized, and students need to be ready. In the rest of this chapter I want to describe a few data- and text-mining methods that can be used right now to begin to make sense of the digitalized information already available.

Geographic Interfaces

Perhaps the most common lament of the history teacher—after complaints about their students' writing—are complaints about how little our students know of or understand about geography, especially historical geography. It might be fashionable to blame GPS devices for turning us into a society of geographic illiterates who cannot read a map to save our lives, preferring instead to just follow the soothing voice of GPS devices, but concerns about student geographic illiteracy did not begin with the appearance of inexpensive directional aids on the market several years ago.[15]

Historians have been worrying about this problem for decades, if not longer.[16] At the most basic level we want students to be able to read a map; to decode some, if not all, of the information it contains; and to understand that a map is a historical source that makes an argument all its own.[17] At a more sophisticated level, we want students to understand that human actions have been constrained or abetted by geographic realities. It is this latter goal that can best be served through digital tools because those tools allow us to create visual representations of historical information that are explicitly linked to geography. These geographic visualization systems can be either quite simple such as creating a layer for Google Earth, or quite complex, using the most sophisticated geographic information processing systems such as those provided by companies like Esri. These latter systems also make it possible to mine large databases of geotagged information to create sophisticated maps of data. Among the simplest examples of how geographic visualizations can be used to help students make sense of events in the past are simple layers created for Google Earth or other similar mapping interfaces. The community of users creating historical layers for Google Earth is quite large, and the number of new layers produced each day continues to grow at a rapid pace.

Students working on a particular research project can be well served by examining the layers available on their particular topic. For instance, a student researching the U2 incident during the Cold War might find his or her way to a Google Earth layer that maps out the diary entries of Frances Gary Powers throughout his career (with a particular emphasis on the period 1958–1962), and includes photographs from Powers's personal collection, as well as approximate route maps for his flights over the Soviet Union.[18] Seeing the events on the globe while reading the diary entries can help our student to understand how the surveillance program had to take into account the great distances involved in overflying the Soviet Union. Because Powers's diary entries are all geolocated, the student researcher can also see his career as a pilot in geographic space, not merely as words on a page. Many, if not most, of the historical layers created for Google Earth exist because amateur historians create them. As a result, encouraging students to use these layers as historical sources without some sort of training in how to pay close attention to what they find there is akin to the problems of turning them loose on search engines discussed in chapter 2. Among the questions they ought to be asking of this particular source include: are the Powers diary entries provided in this layer complete or edited; have all of the diary entries been added to the map layer, or only those that make a point the creator of this map layer wants to make; and who created this resource?

A more sophisticated version of this same sort of project is Light and Shadows: Emma Goldman 1910–1916.[19] This blending of geography and historical sources provides users with a map of the United States with a pin in the map indicating "all the places in America that the anarchist Emma Goldman gave talks, and all the topics she spoke on" between 1910 and 1916. A temporal slider across the bottom of the screen allows users to limit the number of pins in the map to a particular year or even part year. For instance, if the user selects just the year 1910, thirty-six pins are displayed: each of them offering information about one or more of the events on Goldman's schedule. Wherever possible, the project team has embedded links to documents from the Goldman archive, including newspaper stories and texts of lectures given by Goldman. One glance at the map indicates how well travelled Goldman was as a speaker. During 1910 alone, she spoke (or attempted to speak) up and down the West Coast, through the mountain West, across the upper plains, down into Iowa and Missouri, up along the Great Lakes, throughout the Northeast, and down the mid-Atlantic coast as far as Washington, D.C. A student looking at this map might well ask how someone could cover so much territory in the United States in 1910, what forms of transportation she might have used (train, horse, boat), who paid for all that travel, and why Goldman spoke in certain locations and not others? By drilling down even further, one can see that the bulk of Goldman's activities in 1910 took place before the end of June, with almost no speaking engagements in the second half of the year. This finding makes it even more surprising that she could have covered so much territory in just six months, and begs the question of why her speaking trailed off in the second half of the year? The answer to this question is found on the website by clicking on one of the pins for New York City—Goldman was in the hospital (under an assumed name) in the summer of 1910, recovering from a broken kneecap. Or one could look at the site in a different way, focusing on only one location—for example, St. Louis—to see that Goldman spoke or attempted to speak there on twenty-one different occasions, for which the project offers more than thirty related primary sources. Among the lessons students can learn from working with this geographic interface are that transportation was perhaps more efficient than they might have imagined it to be 100 years ago, that politicians often travel to locations where they have willing audiences, that anarchist sentiment seems to have been spread across the United States just after the turn of the twentieth century, and that this sentiment seemed to be clustered in industrial centers.

At a more sophisticated level, historians and geographers have created web-accessible interfaces that allow users to examine large datasets in geographic space. For example, the project NS-Crimes in Vienna offers users the ability to examine a large database on the expulsion of Jews from the Austrian capital after the National Socialist takeover in 1938 either by accessing the data directly, or via a map of the city at that time which shows the concentration of Jews in any given neighborhood.[20] For example, one can learn that until August 1, 1938, Olga Bernstein lived at Pilgerimgasse 22, at which point she was evicted from her home for being Jewish, and was subsequently deported to Minsk in what had been territory of the Soviet Union (now Belarus) on November 28, 1941, with her husband, Juda. We can also learn from the database that Bernstein's maiden name was Fuchs, and that she was born on July 14, 1900, in the former Austrian province of Moravia. Her husband, Juda, was born in Bobrnjsk, Russia, on June 20, 1888. Also, we can see where the Bernsteins lived in the city by clicking over to the map from the database. No date of death is available from the database for either Olga or Juda, so it is unclear from the data available on this website whether either (or both) survived the war. This database, combined with its mapping capabilities, allows users to visualize not only the patterns of Jewish residence in Vienna, but also the patterns of deportation from the city over time. Students examining the map can be prompted to ask questions about the timing of the expulsions—were poor Jews expelled before wealthy Jews (based on the neighborhoods they lived in)—or was the process of clearing Jews from Vienna conducted according to some other logic? By seeing the data in geographic space, students are able to ask questions they cannot ask from the data alone.

An even more sophisticated version of this same type of historical interface is the Digital Harlem project created by Stephen Robertson of the University of Sydney.[21] Where the NS-Crimes project only allows the user to view data from a database in geographic space, Digital Harlem lets the user take a much more active role in the creation of geographic representations of historical data. The user can specify events, people, or places, and create interactive map layers that show how these historical data map onto the geography of Harlem. Thus, a student interested in the history of prostitution in New York City could create a map layer showing arrests for prostitution and another for the locations of brothels in Harlem (fig. 8).

Fig. 8. Digital Harlem: Everyday Life 1915–1930 (http://acl.arts.usyd.edu
.au/harlem) map layers, showing arrests for prostitution and the locations
of brothels in Harlem. Accessed January 11, 2011.

Right away students will see that the locations of brothels and the arrests for prostitution do not correlate very well at all. The brothels are
much closer to midtown Manhattan, while the arrests for prostitution
are clustered much farther uptown. This finding raises historians' questions such as whether the police were working with the brothel owners
in Harlem and so avoided arresting prostitutes close to the brothels, or
conversely, if the police made the blocks around the brothels unfriendly locations for prostitutes to ply their trade, so they stayed further uptown? A

diligent student who did not have access to this map interface could puzzle out the lack of correlation between the locations of brothels and arrests for prostitution by examining the address data for each source. But with the digital interface, she can see how the historical data appear in physical space at the click of a mouse.

While these projects devoted to events in the history of Harlem and Vienna offer users a much richer experience of the historical data than they could have by simply reading sources available in various archives, these projects are still static in nature—by which I mean the user experience is delimited entirely by the website's creators. At the other end of the spectrum is the Hypercities project created at UCLA.[22] Using the Hypercities platform, students and/or other users can build their own interactive maps organized around a particular unit of geography—in this case, one of several cities around the world the project's creators have made available. Once they are logged into the project and have permission to begin adding content, students can mark up the most current satellite image of their city with geotagged data—images, text, sound, or video files—which are then visible on the map via individual pins placed there. Like the Google mapping community overlays, the student-created maps in Hypercities have all the advantages and disadvantages of user-generated content. On the one hand, the items students select for inclusion on a map are reflective of their own interests, and so can be much more interesting to the students themselves. On the other hand, there is a high degree of variability in the quality of what is posted on the maps, and a number of the pins lead to "items" such as "This is where I like to jog." Nevertheless, by handing over a fair amount of control over what is posted to the map interfaces, the creators of the Hypercities project have transferred the locus of control from the website's creators to the website's users—a central element of Web 2.0 interfaces.[23] In doing so, they are turning students loose to become creators of history rather than passive consumers of history. As I have argued throughout the book, giving students this freedom to be creative is an essential element of teaching history in the digital age, but with the caveat that we must also teach them how to make the most of this freedom. Learning to make the best use of the control they are being handed—instead of using that control to post notices about their favorite restaurants or where they jog—is something history students already need to know.

Right now, historians and history students rely on projects such as

those already described to make available limited sets of geotagged historical information. But as more and more historical sources are marked up
with longitude and latitude, we can expect to see more and more and simpler and simpler interfaces for manipulating these datasets. For instance,
it is already about as easy as it could possibly be to use the Yahoo Pipes
platform to access geotagged data from a variety of websites. In just a two-
step process it is possible to select a defined number of geotagged images
from Flickr's database that are geolocated near a particular coordinate on a
map and display them as pins on a map, much like those in the Goldman
project. This simple image-extraction application was created by someone
(me) with virtually no knowledge of programming or computing beyond
the most obvious coding needed to work with a blog or simple webpage.[24]
New applications that make this sort of mapping easier and easier appear
almost monthly. The beta version of a service called "HistoryPin" offers
uses the opportunity to "pin their history to the world" by geotagging any
historical images they own and making them available.[25] For students of
history, such services are blank slates on which they can write their own
versions of the past, and it is very useful not only to let them write on that
slate, but also to critique what those in the public at large have done with
the interface. Are the sources others place on a map properly identified?
How are they described? What can we learn (or not) from what we find on
such sites? How, as historians, can we do a better job?

Text

As interesting as maps are as graphical interfaces for displaying historical data, historians still work most often with text sources, and given the
amount of historical text already online and the ever-growing corpus of
such text, being able to use machine methods for making sense of this massive database of historical text is no longer a luxury—it is an imperative. I
have already suggested ways that historians will eventually have easy access
to recombinant documents that will allow them to look for new relationships between bits or chunks of historical information. But the example
of the Czech politicians relied on the historian already having an idea of
what he or she was looking for; that is, evidence connected in some way
to a particular meeting of political party leaders. But what happens when
the historian instead confronts a database of historical data with much less
well-formed questions, such as "What was the nature of the relationships

between the historical actors in this database?" or "Is there any evidence of change in family patterns over time, and if so, are those changes related at all to patterns in the economy?" or "Did Adolf Hitler's use of anti-Semitic rhetoric vary according to the audiences for his speeches?" or "What was the impact of Spanish Jesuit missions on local economies in colonial Mexico?" These are historians' questions—the kind we ask all the time. But finding answers to such questions, especially when those answers might require us to examine a very large amount of data, is often quite difficult and time consuming. In earlier decades, we have often narrowed the scope of our investigations to what is possible in a given amount of time given the amount of time and support we have to complete a particular project. In 1958, the one-time AHA president David H. Pinkney gave a lecture at the Newberry Library, in which he discussed why it was that American historians of France had been unable to produce magisterial studies comparable to the works of Georges Lefebrve or Albert Soboul. In his lecture, Pinkney blamed

> . . . this failure to the inability of Americans, owing to geographical separation, to do the sustained work in French archives that was the foundation of the great French books. I urged my American colleagues to cease trying to meet our French friends on their own ground with monographs but instead to write on broader subjects that are of interest to Americans concerned with European history and not merely to French historians, to draw on the detailed works of others, and to study in depth in archives only neglected or debated aspects of the subject—a possible task for an American on sabbatical leave and occasional summer research trips.[26]

The problem Pinkney first described in 1958 has been turned on its head by digital technology. Many historians now have ready online access to too many sources on their chosen topic. Instead of worrying about how to gain access to enough sources in order to write books and articles, historians now must contend with a rapidly growing flood of sources—already so great in some cases that we cannot possibly cope with the amount of information available to us without the use of data-processing tools. Of course, this corpus of historical sources is very uneven—rich countries' libraries and archives have been digitizing their collections at a much more rapid rate than poor countries. But the velocity of mass-digitalization projects is growing with each passing year. Cast your mind back ten years and recollect how many online historical sources were available in 2001, and then compare that number to what is available in 2013. Then project that growth forward another ten years, factoring in improvements in scanning techniques, and try to imagine how many online historical sources will be available to students in 2021. Even conservative projections make that number so great that the need to teach students to work with text mining and analysis software seems as obvious in 2013 as Pinkney's advice to his colleagues was in 1958.

One simple example of how text mining can help answer historians' questions is the matter of how to puzzle out relationships between individuals in a particular database. Text-mining algorithms are very good at this important but time-consuming task. In a series of posts in his now-defunct blog *Digital History Hacks (2005–2008)*, the Canadian historian Bill Turkel describes his use of text-mining techniques to compute such relationships in a historical database. Working with a test sample of 100 entries (from the approximately 10,000) in the *Dictionary of Canadian Biography*, Turkel used software to suggest possible relationships between his test group.[27] The results were both unsurprising and surprising. As Turkel points out, he could have anticipated some of the results of this clustering analysis without the aid of the program he wrote, but other relationships suggested by the software were completely puzzling and it was the puzzling results that then required his skill as a historian to analyze. As valuable as it is to confirm what we would have already expected to learn, discovering new information in online sources that would not have been easily accessible through other means points to a significant benefit of text mining.[28] In Turkel's example, his software suggested that there is a relationship between 6 individuals in his test database of 100, but that relationship is not at all obvious at first. The only way to find out what that relationship might be is to delve directly into the data in those six entries, and it is just possible that this research effort might turn up something wholly unexpected. Given that Turkel's program calculated all possible relationships between these 100 individuals in just a few seconds and could have done the same for all 10,000 entries in the *DCB* in around twenty-four hours, one can imagine how quickly historians will soon be able to sort through massive corpuses of text in a short amount of time.

Similarly, one could take a large body of text that is not in database form as in the prior example—for example, a novel like *Les Misérables*—

and with text-mining software determine relationships between the characters, such as how often they interact with one another.[29] Many text-mining products allow the user to see such relationships in a graphical way that may then suggest degrees of interaction not readily apparent on the first reading of the text. Or, in the case of very large bodies of text, information presented in graphical form may make it possible for the reader to focus his or her reading of the text on only certain characters whose relationships seem to be particularly significant. Similarly, it is possible to use these same techniques to examine ideas and their relationship to one another in a corpus of text. For instance, one might take all of Adolf Hitler's speeches during a given electoral campaign and then compare the relationships that might exist between key terms in his rhetoric such as "Jew," "Bolshevik," "race," "economy," and so on. If these speeches were then sorted by type of audience (party gathering, speech to a group of business leaders), regionally, or on the basis of size of metropolitan area, one might then be able to see whether the focus of his campaign rhetoric shifted according to audience or geographic location.[30] Once the user can see such possible relationships, then it is possible to engage in a much more focused reading of the speeches themselves. Software still cannot analyze text in all the ways a historian would, but it can suggest interesting starting points for that analysis, and with each passing year the text mining and analysis algorithms get better and better.[31]

What does this mean for our students and for the teaching of history in the second decade of the twenty-first century? Already, a number of simple tools exist that can be used to introduce students to the possibilities inherent in text mining. While it is not a good idea to rely solely on off-the-shelf word-cloud tools like Many Eyes or Wordle, these tools are easy to learn and can provide a useful introduction to the issues text mining raises for historians.[32] While creating a simple word cloud from a body of text is an easy way to introduce students to the idea of text mining, these visualizations are also useful for demonstrating to them how relying on simple analysis like this can lead to erroneous conclusions like *War and Peace* being all about Russia.[33] However, using this simple tool, students can be introduced to the idea of text mining by uploading a paper they have written and then playing around with the various text-visualization tools. They will see, for instance, how often they use particular words (sometimes comically so). Once introduced to text-mining techniques and the issues they raise for historical analysis, students can then be taught to use much more sophisticated text- and data-mining engines and the visualization software that allows scholars to work with these data in more interesting and productive ways. For example, a slightly more sophisticated tool than the word-cloud packages is Google's NGram viewer, which lets students track and compare the use of various words or phrases over time in the immense database of Google Books. As a simple example, students can track the use of "war" and "peace" in those millions of books and note that, at least in those books currently scanned by Google, "war" overtook "peace" in 1743. This finding, of course, does not mean that war was more popular than peace beginning in 1743, but rather, can point students toward productive questions about why war would be more commonly used than peace, and why by the twentieth century the difference in frequency between the two words would become so pronounced.[34]

Among the issues students need to be aware of is that using text mining on subtle forms of speech like political rhetoric can be a tricky proposition. Text mining works best when the text being examined by the software follows a particular set of well-defined rules. So, for instance, Dan Cohen created a simple text-mining tool he called "Syllabus Finder" in 2003 to search the Internet for course syllabi.[35] Course syllabi generally follow a basic set of rules, regardless of discipline, which include text such as the professor's name, the title of the course, the meeting pattern of the course, a course number, and things with names like "office hours," "required readings," etc. Using these text identifiers, Cohen was able to mine the Internet for syllabi for a number of years until Google discontinued access to the API the Syllabus Finder required.[36]

A political speech, however, may or may not follow a well-defined or easily discernible set of rules that makes it amenable to text mining. In the American context, for instance, oppositional terms such as "pro-choice/pro-life," or "gun rights/gun control" may indicate the ideological position of a particular speaker, but politicians can also be much more subtle in their speech. For instance, this passage from a speech given in the U.S. Senate in 2003 by Senator Patty Murray expresses her opposition to a bill known as the "Partial-Birth Abortion Ban Act of 2003."

Since we began debating how to criminalize women's health choices yesterday, the Dow Jones has dropped 170 points; we are 1 day closer to a war in Iraq; we have done nothing to stimulate the economy or create any new jobs or provide any more health coverage.[37]

Anyone familiar with the parameters of the American debate over abortion rights will be able to tell that the phrase "debating how to criminalize women's health choices" is a clear statement of opposition to limitations on abortion rights, but a text-mining algorithm looking for the pro-choice/pro-life pairing might well miss this particular nuance. It is certainly possible to tweak algorithms so that they produce much more sophisticated analyses of complex texts such as speeches in the U.S. Senate, but as historians come to rely more and more on such algorithms to search massive text corpuses, we will first have to learn how to do this tweaking on our own.[38] Once we know how to do it, we will then have to figure out the best ways to teach students to do the same thing. From the simple example of Senator Murray's speech from 2003, one can see that even with the best algorithms, historians will still need to read a certain number of primary sources in detail to make sure we have taken an inclusive view of the text identifiers the algorithm should be searching for. As mentioned earlier, anyone familiar with the parameters of the American debate on abortion rights can tell which side Senator Murray was on in 2003. But what would the text identifiers be in letters written between various representatives of the Spanish crown in South and Central America around 1800, or Chinese provincial governors around 1700? As with American political speech in the twenty-first century, the historian would need to know the letter writing conventions and the key vocabulary of Spanish or Chinese officials in order to properly instruct the algorithm as it scans all those texts. Our historian (or history student) must teach the algorithm how to search through a database of these letters, and to do that he or she must first understand that parameters of the political debate in the Spanish and Chinese empires at the time, and know how those parameters were expressed in language. Only then can text mining proceed successfully.

The ability to teach an algorithm how to search across thousands or tens of thousands of official documents more than two centuries old is, fortunately, a skill historians already possess and teach our students. We know how to make sense of these language conventions and for decades we have been teaching students how to read the same documents we read. By the end of the current decade it is a safe assumption that sophisticated data- and text-mining tools will be much more user friendly, and so therefore accessible to novice learners. If this assumption is correct, now is the time we need to develop, test, and refine teaching strategies that will incorporate these tools as they emerge. Otherwise students will either try to use these tools on their own with limited or mixed results, or, more likely, will not use them at all, and the degree they receive will be ever more outdated.

Image Mining

The other large category of historical sources that historians rely on is images. Sorting through the seemingly limitless databases of historical images is currently a very inefficient process. The user must either use a search engine such as the Google or Yahoo image search, which returns images in an order that is not particularly useful, or must already know which database to search through to find what he or she is looking for (e.g., American Memory). In either case, the student conducting the search is dependent upon the metadata added to images for either type of search to work at all. Because the object of data mining is to turn up new information not readily available in other ways and to provide analysis of that information, this sort of image browsing does not qualify as "image mining."

Mining visual sources for usable information is much trickier than the mining of text for several reasons. The most important of these is that while text follows the sorts of rules discussed earlier (grammar, structure of the text, etc.), images follow very few rules that can be used in historical-data mining. Among the few objective bits of information common to all images are size of the image and the makeup of the pixels in that digital image; that is, how many blue, how many red, and what the density of those pixels is in any particular quadrant of the image. These sorts of basic data provide some information that is usable for humanists, and certainly even this limited amount of data will lead to the creation of new knowledge about the content of the images.[39] For now, though, we lack clear intersections between the underlying data—size, pixels—that can be extracted from the image and the meanings that can be made from interpretation of the content of the image, sometimes known as the "semantic gap."[40] This gap in meaning making—one that those working in the field of text mining are beginning to bridge already—is really no more than an engineering problem that will be overcome soon enough. This particular engineering problem is more difficult to deal with because we do not yet even have a reliable way to locate images that are related to one another across multiple databases absent metadata providing those links. However, software designers are beginning to make progress when it comes to this latter task. It is already possible to train a search algorithm to ferret out images of a particular object—a motorcycle, for instance—by determining which sectors of the image of a motorcycle might be indicative of images of any motorcycle. Once several such sectors have been identified, then the algorithm can assume that any image it scans that contains a sufficient number of matches for those sectors must be (or at least is likely to be) a motorcycle.[41] Already this technology is being used to combat online child pornography by identifying images that might include not only children, but sexual content.[42]

This very rudimentary process of identifying objects such as motorcycles is but the first step toward a much more robust capability to search databases of historical images. Imagine for a moment what it will be like when a student working on a paper on the diffusion of steam technology in the nineteenth century is able to search across a cluster of large databases of historical images for possible images of a particular model of steam engine. If the software is sufficiently robust, it might also be possible to identify different models of the same engine based upon unique characteristics of the engine itself, if such details are present in an image. Depending on the metadata available for the various images returned in such a search (date, location, image creator, etc.) it may well be possible to do such things as map out the locations of these steam engines and the dates they were photographed. Seeing the diffusion of this particular technology over time and space may suggest new questions, new answers, or simply new avenues for investigation to students. Or, instead of an industrial product like a steam engine, what if students were working on images of a particular public figure (artist, politician, social reformer) and could use the software to ferret out all images of that figure? What might be learned from such information? What new questions might be generated? Or what if a student was interested in the use of a particular image in books, magazines, and digital media? Take for instance, an iconic photograph like Dorothea Lange's *Migrant Mother*, which appears in hundreds, if not thousands, of books and articles, and on countless websites.[43] Because Lange's 1936 image of Florence Owens Thompson and her children is a singular item, searching algorithms can be trained to locate this item with much greater ease, and can return such additional data as the title of the book where the image was located, the page number, author, date of publication, and so on. We are still a way off from mining images in these ways, but given what is already possible with existing algorithms, these same scenarios might be possible in as little as five years. Given that students may very well be able to engage in this kind of image mining soon, it is incumbent upon us as educators to begin working on ways to train them to do this sort of sophisticated work.

How will our students survive and prosper as historians in a world with millions of books, and billions of other sources available online at the click of a mouse? They will do so only if historians begin to take seriously the need to train students to work with not only the vast quantities of historical information now available to them, but also with the increasingly sophisticated software tools under development for working with those resources. To do that, of course, we have to learn to use these tools ourselves so that we can develop useful models for students: teaching and learning exercises that help them make sense of the huge online library of historical resources. Finally, we need to begin thinking carefully as a community of scholars about the kinds of historical questions one can reasonably ask of these super-massive databases. Once we have a better handle on what those questions are and how we might go about answering them, then we can engage students in a lively discussion about both the questions and the possible answers. Because students often have technology skills that are substantially greater than our own, inviting them to be part of this discussion will almost certainly be well worth the effort.

< 4 >

Presenting

Capturing, Creating, and Writing History

History and writing are inseparable. We cannot know
history well unless we write about it.
—Richard Marius,
A Short Guide to Writing About History (1995)

Form and content can be separated.
—Michael Wesch,
"Web 2.0 . . . The Machine is Us/ing Us" (2007)

Since Herodotus first began scratching out his *Histories* almost 2,500 years
ago, historians have been writing about the past. Text and history have
been inseparable companions for all the centuries since the Persian wars,
and thanks to the Chinese, for almost 2,000 years, we have been writing
those texts on paper. With a little help from Herr Gutenberg, for more
than half a millennium we have been writing those histories in mass-
produced books and other forms made possible by moveable type and
the printing press. For much of the last hundred years or so, those books,
articles, conference papers, and other forms of academic historical writing
have followed a form easily recognizable to today's readers. Books have a
title and an author or authors, and usually have a table of contents, page
numbers, (often) an index, and if the author uses footnotes or endnotes
those notes adhere to one of several generally accepted formats (Chicago,
MLA, etc.), and books are almost always divided into chapters.[1] Journal
articles, papers, and other forms of historical writing adhere to many of

78

these same forms, leaving out only the organizational features such as the table of contents. Historians continue to write in these same ways, but we also now write blogs, e-books that were never intended for print, journal articles that appear only online, headnotes for database entries, have Twitter feeds, create music videos, and produce other forms of electronic historical writing that looks and feels quite different from the books and articles that have been the staple of the discipline for the past century. New online platforms that aggregate content from various of these sources into something not quite a journal, not quite a book, not quite a website.[2] Increasing numbers of historians are embracing the possibilities of digital media for creating history when it comes to their own work, but there is not much evidence that these changes have worked their way into the history classroom.

While the forms of our writing about the past have begun to change only recently, the style of our writing evolved significantly beginning in the 1950s. For all the centuries up to the most recent one, historical writing was largely narrative in style, but since the Second World War analytical forms have mostly pushed aside narrative historical writing in the academy. Where once history was part of the humanities and historians were considered great writers in their own right, now the historical profession is much more likely to reward analytical sophistication over a good story.[3] Of course, the market still rewards a good story and many an excellent historian has made a fine living writing in less analytical ways for a wider audience. But by and large, we demand from one another and from our students, written text that is precise, analytical, and that is embedded in the larger interplay of historical work we call scholarship. We are so used to writing about the past, we are so much a text-based professional culture, that we almost always expect our students to replicate what we do adhering as closely to the forms we know and are comfortable with as possible. History students write innumerable essays before they graduate from college, and if asked they will happily tell you that these essays are of a type. The content changes from course to course, but their professors' expectation of the form of the five-, seven-, or ten-page essay is largely consistent across the curriculum. Is it any wonder some of them get bored, especially since the ways they "write" in the rest of their lives are so different?[4]

Think for just a minute about the quotation from Richard Marius cited at the outset of this chapter. Is it really possible that "history and writing are inseparable"? Or that "We cannot know history well unless we write about it"? If that is true and Marius is right, the historical profession has two choices: change our ideas about what it means for our students to "write" about the past, or fade into irrelevance. If you do not believe me, consider the results of a survey 200 students in Michael Wesch's Cultural Anthropology class at Kansas State University conducted on themselves in the fall of 2007. After analyzing one another, those students determined that in that year they would read eight books, 2,300 web pages, and 1,281 Facebook profiles. In the fall semester they would write 42 pages for various classes, but 500 pages of email.[5] Now consider that these students surveyed themselves in 2007, not 2012. As ubiquitous as Facebook was in 2007, it had not yet achieved its current almost total capture of the American undergraduate student population.[6] These data also do not capture the thousands of text messages the average college student will write in a single semester. As mentioned in chapter 1, a substantial fraction of those 2,300 web pages will offer up hundreds or perhaps thousands of hours of video they will watch on their computers. A substantial fraction of today's students will have a blog; a Twitter feed; will publish and mark up photographs; will insert tags on images, videos, blog posts, and Facebook profiles; will create online videos; and will write entries for databases. And perhaps many will write comments ranging from a few words to many hundreds on content they find online.[7]

None, or at least very little, of this "writing" they do on various websites and in various media has anything to do with what we call academic historical writing—at least from the standpoint of form. What they say may be said in precise, analytical language, but more likely it is going to be casual in tone and form. Does that make it less insightful? Perhaps, but not always. This chapter considers how, going forward from 2013, we need to think very carefully about how to teach students to organize, make sense of, and present history in the intermediated world they inhabit.[8] My purpose is not to argue that the five-page essay is dead as a form of historical writing in the college course—even though to our students it may already be their version of Banquo's ghost—dead, but annoyingly haunting. Instead, I suggest a number of ways to think about how students can and will represent the results of their historical investigations in a variety of forms, only one of which is the essay. Writing a solid historical essay is still a very important skill that students need to develop, but it is also incumbent upon us as their teachers and mentors to help them mine these various forms of presenting historical information for all they are worth, while helping them remain true to the values of our profession.

Before we proceed to the forms historical presentation is taking and likely will take in the future, we should first consider the purposes behind requiring students to present their analysis of the past in any form other than the spoken word. There are several very good reasons why we demand these concrete representations of the past from our students. The first of these is the one Marius asserts in the quotation cited earlier in this chapter. Whether it be writing, creating a poster, a website, a short film, a blog, an interactive map, or some other form of the representation of historical investigation, one thing we have learned over the years is that asking students to take the evidence they have gathered and put it into a form that makes that evidence intelligible to others spurs new ideas and reinforces memories other than those that take place during the investigatory stage of historical work. The act of figuring out how to organize the results of our investigations and analysis into a form that makes sense to other people forces us to think about our sources, our data, and the results of our analysis in different ways than we would otherwise. Because students must also consider their audience—whether it be the professor, the rest of the students in a classroom, or anyone online who finds their way to something the student has posted online—a certain amount of critical thinking must also take place about how the information contained in the presentation will be seen, read, and understood. Neuroscientists argue persuasively that there is a cognitive gain that accrues from the act of preparing information to be presented to others and so we are onto something good when we force students to represent their thinking in concrete forms.

We want our students to be literate, to be knowledgeable about the past, to be able to present the results of their research in clear and precise ways, and we believe, the papers we ask them to write and the other forms of representation we demand will help prepare them for various forms of writing and presenting they will have to do after they graduate. It is true that unless they go on to graduate school, few of our alumni will ever write another five-page essay. Nevertheless, it is also the case that any number of professions expect some form of writing, and so we comfort ourselves with the knowledge (or the assumption) that those many papers we require will help students in their future careers. If employers are to be believed, then we are not wrong in these assumptions. A January 2010 study published by the American Association of Colleges and Universities surveyed employers in the United States about their views on the role of higher education in preparing students for success in the new economy. At the top of the list of intellectual and practical skills that employers wanted students to gain in college was "The ability to communicate effectively, orally and in writing." Also near the top of their list were critical-thinking and analytical-reasoning skills, the ability to collaborate with others, problem-solving skills, the ability to innovate and be creative, and complex research skills (finding and evaluating information from multiple sources).[9] The employers responding to this survey also placed great emphasis on the need for students to complete some sort of significant project in their major prior to graduation that makes use of the skills of their discipline, to take part in an internship or field-based research experience "to connect classroom learning with real-world experience," and to learn both research skills and the ability to engage in evidence based analysis. What the employers surveyed specifically did not stipulate, is how these various skills should be acquired. Given that so few of them expect their employees to write analytical essays, I think it is fair to say that students need a diversity of writing experiences prior to graduation to prepare them for the world they will face after receiving their diploma.[10]

In today's workplace, how often do professionals have to commit 1,000 or more words to paper or pixels? Attorneys, intelligence analysts, and others certainly write many pages of text each year. But how many words does a high school teacher, a web-content manager, or an advertising professional commit to paper or pixels from year to year? Those who find themselves in these roles are much more likely to have to write smaller chunks of text for websites, company blogs, for examination review sheets, or for an annual report. Anyone who has written for the web knows that web writing is very different from the sort of writing I am doing now as I write this book. Where books, articles, and five-page papers put a premium on spinning out an argument in detail, writing for the web—as more and more of our alumni will do once they graduate—depends on being able to create a "chunk" of text that is pithy, informative, and short. These chunks may someday be assembled into something published, such as a book or an article, but the much more likely result of the web writing our alumni do will be little more than a disconnected corpus of chunks of text.[11] This reality then begs the question of whether the five-page paper really helps students prepare for the world they will live in once they graduate? My belief is that it does not. The longer we insist that students represent the results of their research in a form that was as ubiquitous in 1977 when I was a college freshman as it is today, the more likely it will be that we will be stewards of a profession increasingly out of sync with the realities of the lives students lead, or plan to lead, after graduation. In an educational world driven increasingly by cost-benefit analyses, clinging to increasingly traditional forms of representation such as the five-page paper as the primary way students represent the results of their learning seems riskier with each passing year.

One reason why writing remains important as one of the many ways students can provide evidence of their learning is that there is an important evaluative component to the writing we assign. We demand that students write about their work so we can evaluate their efforts and understanding in ways we are very familiar and comfortable with. By the time most teachers hit the classroom as the teacher/professor of record, they have had some significant experience with grading student essays. From what the student wrote, most of us can answer questions such as whether the author's research was thorough? Is the analysis based on evidence or mere conjecture? Did the author embed his or her analysis in the preexisting conversation among historians? Does the conclusion proceed clearly from their data and analysis, and so on. By answering these questions we can evaluate their efforts and their understanding of the lessons we want them to learn. The feedback they receive from us helps to reinforce lessons learned during the investigatory and representative phases of their work. This submission/feedback loop also makes it possible for us to assign a grade for the students' work.

Until recently, the submission/feedback loop in history education was a very private matter. Students turned in their work to their professors, and the professors evaluated the work and gave it back with comments and a numeric or letter grade. Sometimes the rest of the class might engage in group evaluation of one another's work, but those instances have been exceptions rather than the rule. In the world students live in now, they receive all sorts of feedback on a daily basis. Friends "like" items posted on Facebook pages, they comment on photographs or videos posted on various websites, they rank contributions to databases, and generally engage in a constant back and forth with one another over the things they post online. Research on student success in college indicates that the more they collaborate with one other (rather than with their professor) in the learning process, the more likely they are to be successful.[12] When we ask students to create historical work in a digital environment, we create the possibility for greater collaboration between the students in the course and, depending upon the digital environment we choose, with others not enrolled in the course—students in other sections of the course, students enrolled at other institutions, or the public at large. However, simply creating the opportunity for such online collaboration does not *ipso facto* mean student work will improve. In fact, instructors who create collaborative environments for students and then just expect the students to take full advantage of those opportunities, are often quite disappointed with the results. The reason for this disappointment is not difficult to find. As mentioned earlier, today's students are adept users of technology, but they are only rarely adept learners with the technology. As a result, we need to teach them how to make the best use of the opportunities we create for them— how to comment constructively on one another's work, how to create tagging systems that make sense, how to build communities of practice, not just friend networks.[13] Similarly, our students need to learn how to act and react, how to write and rewrite, when the boundaries of the classroom expand to take in the world at large. This expansion of the classroom happens, at least potentially, every time they post some of their work online in a place others not enrolled in the course can see it.

If the five-, seven-, or ten-page essay is no longer to be the primary standard expectation of history students, then what else should we expect of them, and what should they expect from us, going forward from 2012? In chapter 1, I offered a list of historical thinking skills that we want to inculcate in students before they graduate. When we think about the goals of history education, we typically combine a list such as mine with a list of content knowledge that we think every history major should know (or every student in a particular course should know). Most historians agree in general terms on lists of thinking skills, but debates over what content to teach and/or emphasize are and will remain quite lively. I submit that we need to include a third list—practical skills—that give students the opportunity to make use of the historical thinking skills they are learning in a digital environment conducive to the making of history. Such environments can include gallery or museum exhibits (analog or virtual), oral histories, the creation of historical websites or videos, public presentations at conferences or other similar venues, group projects that result in a tangible product—something that lives on beyond the end of the course—or a database of historical information made available to a wider audience. For example, in 2009, one of my students created an art exhibition from a series of photographs taken in Berlin as the Berlin Wall was being built. This exhibition, *Halt!* Grenze, taught her not only how to create a historical exhibition from primary sources, but also how to present that work online as part of a larger project on the twentieth anniversary of the fall of the wall.[14] This list does not exhaust the possibilities of the practical work students could be doing, but rather is intended to suggest some of the ways we can help students "make history," rather than just write it. Making history in this way has many tangible benefits to students over and above any learning gains that might accrue. History making gives students the opportunity to explore tangible creative historical products that they can show graduate admissions committees and future employers.

Students certainly derive a sense of satisfaction from the completion of (and grade from) a well-written historical essay, and are almost certainly better for having written such an essay. But what happens to that essay once the graded version is handed back by the professor? Do students publish those essays online for others to read? Do they hand out copies to their friends? Most often, they file the graded essay away, and at some point later in life recycle the paper. The process of writing an essay, handing it in, having a grade assigned, and receiving it back from the professor is most often a project that involves only two people and is almost entirely private. No one benefits from the process but the student writing the essay. By contrast, if the student creates history in the ways that historians create history (other than writing books or articles), entering his or her work into the public discussion about the past, then the work the student does is no longer part of a binary and private exchange with a professor. Instead, he or she has done what we insist our colleagues do—make the work public so that others can use it or comment on it. This sort of public back and forth is certainly possible in other ways—making multiple copies of a paper and passing it around to others in the room—the technology available to us now simply makes the process easier.

For example, in the spring 2011 semester, I rewrote my Historical Methods course with the specific intention of creating more opportunities for my students to *make* history while they were learning about history. Several developments intersected to prompt this rewrite of the course: my conviction that the way we most typically teach methods to students is not especially interesting to them or to us, does not sufficiently take into account the changes that digital media have wrought on our profession, does not place enough emphasis on real, archival research, and, because my research expertise is in Central and Eastern European history, few (if any) of my students could do any original research in the sources I use in my own work. For all these reasons, I decided to create a version of the methods course that would get my students out of the classroom and into the field, would force them into the archives, and would require them to "make history" as a condition of completion of the course. To put it another way, I rebuilt the course around the idea that the best way to teach historical methods was to have students be historians. In doing so, I was responding, in part, to a 2001 critique of history education by the Canadian historian Chad Gaffield.

> In the history courses I took in school in the 1960s, we read about history, talked about history and wrote about history; we never actually did history. If I had learned basketball in this way, I would have spent years reading the interpretations and viewpoints of great players, watching them play games, and analysing the results of various techniques and strategies. Instead, though, I was soon dribbling a basketball and trying to shoot it into the hoop after just a few instructions. In my history courses, by contrast, I did not begin to do any historical research until the end of my undergraduate years, and even in master's seminars, the focus was still on learning about the various viewpoints of historians, rather than directly coming to grips with the past. In basketball terms, I began in earnest to play the sport only at the doctoral thesis level.[15]

While Gaffield, currently the president of Canada's Social Science and Humanities Research Council, is describing the history classes he experienced as a young student in the 1960s, it is not an exaggeration to say that historical methods is still largely taught this same way on most college campuses.

In an attempt to break away from this style of teaching the methods course and to give my students a chance to "play the sport" of history, I created a new version of the old methods course and called it "Dead in Virginia." In creating this new course I took advantage of several opportunities available to my students near my university—George Mason University—located in Fairfax County, Virginia. In Fairfax County, there are more than 400 family cemeteries, and in the surrounding region the number probably approaches 1,000. These cemeteries range in size from a single headstone or marker, to large plots with a few dozen graves. They are in various states of repair or disrepair, and some are more accessible than others: some were within walking distance of campus, others were much farther away; some were located on public lands; others were on private property, but all of them were available for my students as sites of research. In addition to this physical landscape of the past, the local public library's Virginia Room contains vertical files on all of the known family cemeteries in Fairfax County, giving my students access to a real historical archive within walking distance of our campus. Finally, my students were able to connect with representatives of a local historical society—the Fairfax County Cemetery Preservation Association—and so learned the value of the work being done by historians outside the academy.[16] One of the best lessons they learned was that the members of the association had very detailed knowledge of local history, but did not always have equally detailed knowledge of the broader historiography of eighteenth-, nineteenth-, or twentieth-century America.

To complete their work, the students in my class had to select one of the family cemeteries in our local area, go to it, and learn everything they could learn at the site itself—geographic location, orientation, size, condition, number of headstones, number of depressions that might indicate the presence of a grave, information inscribed on the headstones, and so on. While there they had to draw an accurate map of the site and photograph it, along with each of the headstones. Once they had gathered all the information they could at the site, they had to go to the local library and begin their archival research on the cemetery and the people buried there (or suspected to be buried there). Following their archival research, they then turned to online genealogical resources such as Ancestry.com and other primary sources (online and analog) such as newspapers from the time when the people buried in their cemeteries were alive, property and trial records at the local courthouse, and other similar archival sources. Many of the students also tracked down descendants of those buried in their cemeteries and interviewed them, which required them to learn oral history techniques and about university standards for human subjects research. All the source material they gathered then went into a database that would eventually be made public for general use.[17]

Up to this point, their work was decidedly not digital, but from this moment in the semester, their work shifted to almost completely online. In that database they not only had to create individual items for each source they collected using proper archival metadata (built on the Dublin Core standards), they also had to wrestle with all sorts of issues including the definition of fair use; how to resize photographs to dimensions that work on the web; how to geolocate their sources; and how to write descriptive text for the web that is brief, pithy, accurate, and useful to other researchers. Once all their entries were in the database, they then had to investigate the historiography of our area to see what historians have had to say about what was happening when the people buried in cemeteries lived and died. Their final project was to create an online exhibit from their entries and present it to the class in a ten-minute talk. While their final presentations varied in quality (as one would expect in an undergraduate course), one piece of evidence that my students took to being historians while learning historical methods is that while each student was required to place 10 entries in the database, the 19 students in my class created not 190, but 742 entries during the course of the semester. At the time of this writing, two of my students have found additional opportunities to be historians as a result of the work they did in class. One student was asked to write up her work for the June 2011 newsletter of the Fairfax County Park Authority, and another had planned to work as a summer intern at the Virginia Outdoor Foundation to work on the history of a nineteenth-century cemetery recently discovered on land owned by the foundation until a paying job came her way.[18] All of the students spent fourteen weeks being historians—an opportunity we give them too rarely—and because the work they did in the class is now public, that work will live on beyond the grade they received at the end of the semester. The most important outcome of the course, from my perspective anyway, is that the students in my class now understand better what it means to be a historian—everything from how we conceptualize a research project, to how we do the research necessary to complete that project, to how we embed the results of our research in a discussion among scholars, to how we make our work public for others to use. This much more active approach to historical learning and history making—more active anyway than writing a series of essays—generated much more enthusiasm for historical methods than I have ever seen, and led to some very in-depth conversations about what otherwise might have seemed to be arcane rules or practices of the historical profession. Did they learn more about historical methods than they might have otherwise? They may or may not have learned more or learned "better." What I do know is that they learned differently

This redesign of the historical methods course followed a process that Grant Wiggins and Jay McTighe call "backwards design."[19] In their book, *Understanding by Design,* Wiggins and McTighe provide a simple model for rewriting any course to refocus it on understanding rather than coverage, arguing that the best way to engage in such a redesign is to begin at the end of the course and then work one's way back to the beginning.[20] This "backward design" approach requires the instructor to very clear in his or her mind about is what students should know and be able to do at the end of the semester. Once the instructor is clear on the desired outcomes of the course, then he/she decides what will constitute sufficient evidence that the students have achieved those results. Only when the desired results and the acceptable evidence are clearly defined should the instructor plan the learning experiences with those final outcomes and evidence in mind. Too often, we plan our courses based on a desire to make sure our students know all they should know about, say, nineteenth-century Europe, without first pausing to ask what they ought to understand about nineteenth-century Europe? Once we know those things, then—and only then—can we decide how to teach these things and how students will demonstrate their mastery of the concepts, information, and skills that we have built our course around. I think it is safe to say that very few history teachers who made such a list would have "Be able to write an effective five-page paper" at or near the top of their list. However, a five-page paper may well be one of several ways students demonstrate their mastery of the subject. But in the digital world students live in today and will work in tomorrow, we need to be alive to the possibility that there are many other ways they can demonstrate that mastery than yet another essay.

What, then, are some of those ways students can demonstrate mastery of a historical event, development, controversy, person, or other piece of the larger subject matter in a course? Writing about the past remains central to our discipline, but in the digital world students live in, "writing" takes many forms. As Michael Wesch points out in his video "The Machine is Us/ing Us," in the world of Web 2.0, driven by XML rather than HTML, form and content are now separated from one another.[21] In the world of written/printed text that generation after generation of historians has lived in, text was a linear thing—words on a page in a specific order defined by grammar and printing conventions. But in the digital world, that linearity has broken down. First HTML introduced the idea of hyperlinking texts—allowing users to jump from one web page or block of text to another without respect for the rules of grammar, printing, or reading. But, as discussed earlier, with XML, data—whether images, text, census data, video, sound files, or other forms of historical information—can now be stored in a database and used in whatever way the user chooses.

So, for instance, the students in my historical methods course placed 742 items in a database devoted to family cemeteries in our local community. Each student created an online exhibit drawn from his or her own entries that presented his or her family cemetery to the rest of the class. But because the data in the database is freely accessible to all, my students could have used one another's items in their exhibits, or could have created an entirely different exhibit—one that focused on graves of children, or on the graves of Civil War veterans, or any number of other possible choices; just as easily, they could have incorporated items from the database into a video presentation, an essay (online or on paper), or a poster presentation. Because the content and the form were separate from the very beginning of their project, the possibilities for presenting the past were not quite endless, but certainly much more varied than was possible twenty or even ten years ago. What follows are several examples of ways historians have begun to use digital media to expand the options for their students to make history from the raw material they find in their classes, in their reading, and in their research.

Slideware

If it seems to American college students that PowerPoint has existed their entire lives, that is because it has. The first version of what we now know as the world's most dominant presentation software (slideware) appeared on the market as a product for the Macintosh computer in 1987, with the Windows version first available in 1990. Although alternatives to PowerPoint do exist (Keynote, Prezi, Open Office), the product Microsoft purchased from its developers for only $14 million dominates its market segment like almost no other software product. Moreover, these other packages, each of which has its own strengths and weaknesses vis-à-vis PowerPoint, share with Microsoft's product a reductionist approach to information that is foreign to the ways historians think about and present their work. Only Prezi departs from the standard march of one slide after another by giving the user many different ways to organize his or her research on screen. Nevertheless, anyone who has spent any time in a high school or college classroom knows that PowerPoint has assumed a dominating place in the teaching and learning of history as well. One would be hard-pressed to find a high school or college history department where no one uses PowerPoint or other forms of slideware in their teaching.

If you have ever had the opportunity to wander the halls of a high school or college to peek in and see what is happening in the various history classrooms, when you found a classroom with PowerPoint in use, you likely would see a room full of students staring at a slide on the screen (probably a slide with bullet points), either taking notes or just staring at the slide while the professor talked. That classroom was probably devoid of activity other than the professor's voice and the scratching of pens on paper, or the sound of keys being tapped on a laptop or two. Teachers who teach this way are not exceptions. How many meetings have you attended where someone spoke while clicking through PowerPoint slides? How active was the audience in that meeting? According to Edward Tufte, Power-Point is the enemy of active learning, because it "elevates format over content, betraying an attitude of commercialism that turns everything into a sales pitch," and imposes a cognitive style on the speaker and the audience that reduces complex ideas and information to a series of bulleted summaries.[22] Given what has already been discussed in this book about the failure of lectures to elicit the types of learning we want from students, it should be no surprise that using PowerPoint (or other similar presentation software) further reduces the likelihood that the kind of learning we want is going to take place. For one thing, thinking like a historian requires a reasonably high degree of cognitive flexibility, largely because the amount of evidence we have to decipher and the multiple forms that evidences comes in, requires us (and our students) to be able to think across boundaries, to be comfortable with ambiguity and contradiction, and to be creative when marshaling evidence in our solutions to pressing problems about the past.[23] PowerPoint presentations offer none of this flexibility, and do not admit themselves to ambiguity in large part because they are so linear. The professor using slideware to make a presentation in class is locked into the forward motion of the program, moving inexorably from one slide to the next, with little opportunity for diversion or digression without leaving the program to use some other software. If you have ever watched students using printed PowerPoint slides for the purpose of studying, you'll see that they too move inexorably from slide to slide on the page, endeavoring earnestly to memorize the content of the bullet points or the images. Only the most skilled practitioners of PowerPoint can do more than arrange content in the linear manner dictated by the software.

The pedagogical assumptions built into PowerPoint also reinforce two models of history teaching that are detrimental to the kind of learning we want taking place. The first of these is the coverage model that, as Lendol Calder argues, works against students achieving understanding in a course.[24] PowerPoint provides the instructor with the illusion that he or she is imparting piles of useful knowledge to students because that knowledge has appeared on a slide on the screen at the front of the room. Of course, just because information flashed up on the screen, was discussed briefly by the instructor, and then gave way to more information does not mean it was learned. Likely the opposite is true, but the illusion of learning is maintained because the students take notes and are nodding. The second problem with the pedagogical assumptions built into PowerPoint is that it reinforces the notion that there exists some number of "correct" answers to any historical question. Unlike the mathematical, physical, or life sciences, history does not admit to such notions except to a very limited degree. Historians agree, for instance, that the Japanese attacked Pearl Harbor on December 7, 1941, or that Charles I followed James I as the second of the Stuart kings of England. Thus, "December 7, 1941," is the correct answer if a student is asked on what date the Japanese attacked Pearl Harbor on an exam. But the more difficult question of why the Japanese decided to stage a surprise attack on the United States in December 1941 does not admit itself to one clear "correct" answer in the same way that nursing students need to know that humans have two kidneys and one liver, as opposed to the reverse. PowerPoint slides reinforce the notion that there are correct answers that simply must be memorized in order to do well in a history class.

Given these problems induced by the use of slideware in the teaching and learning of history, you might expect that I would argue that we should ban PowerPoint from our classrooms. As tempting as that would be, I think that as educators and as historians we have an obligation to our students to teach them to use PowerPoint and/or other slideware programs to present information to a larger audience, largely because so many professional contexts expect this skill. However, the best corporate uses of PowerPoint are not the slogging progression from one list of bullet points to the next. Instead, they are very, very brief, involve a great deal of motion and change on each slide, and are at least a bit more immersive than the standard-issue classroom PowerPoint presentation. For instance, several years ago, two of my colleagues and I were asked to prepare a presentation for a major telecommunications firm interested in the possibility of hiring our center to create what we would now call "history apps" for the mobile phones in their network. As we discussed the format for the presentation, the marketing manager we were working with said, "When you have your three PowerPoint slides ready, shoot them to me in an email so I can look them over before your presentation." None of us had ever seen a Power-Point presentation with only three slides, and at first had a difficult time imagining how we might construct something compelling enough to convince a big corporation to invest tens of thousands of dollars in our idea. The limit of three slides meant that we had to come up with something entirely different than what we had been thinking we would do. What we learned from that experience was just how important it is to teach students to develop much more sophisticated skills with slideware than we currently teach them.

Given that corporate uses of slideware are so different, what must we do to teach students how to make the most of this resource that they likely must use after graduation and that we are not very good with? The answer lies in our century or more of experience with the five-page paper. Over the decades, historians have evolved a reasonably well-accepted set of notions about how a good history essay should be constructed and most of us teach those notions to our students. What is needed now is a similar set of notions about how PowerPoint and other slideware should be used to communicate to an audience about the past. Rather than relying on the built in templates or "wizards" provided by the software, we should teach students to create their own templates—templates that use no bullet points, that do not summarize crucial information in ways that trivialize the content, that highlight the ambiguity, the conditionality of that past. As Tufte argues, "Presentations largely stand or fall on the quality, relevance, and integrity of the content."[25] We need to teach students how to focus on the quality, relevance, and integrity of the content of their presentations, and then how to use the tools provided to them by the software to create a few dynamic slides that communicate that information in ways that are engaging, thought provoking, and useful to their intended audience, rather than doing something like reducing the Gettysburg Address to a few slides.[26]

Blogs and Microblogs

Blogs and microblogs such as Twitter are increasingly popular forms of social interaction online for college students and, albeit to a significantly lesser degree, their history professors. Blogs—a platform for writing in reverse-date order—first appeared on the Internet in their current form in the late 1990s. Once several free and easy-to-use blogging platforms (Blogger, Wordpress, LiveJournal) became widely available, blogging took off as a form of communication to the point where blogs have become ubiquitous in a variety of contexts—especially news, politics, and entertainment—even as they retain their primary appeal as a form of individual communication with the world as an online journal. No one knows just how many blogs exist, but according to the website blogpulse.com on October 12, 2010, there were 148,156,488—of which more than 80,000 had been created in the past twenty-four hours, and these blogs had generated more than 1 million distinct posts in that same twenty-four-hour period. While Facebook's wall and status fields are not the same thing as a blog, they serve many of the same purposes—updating readers on events, ideas, and feelings of the person whose page is being read. Microblogging platforms such as Twitter, once the province of the over-twenty cohort, have made significant inroads into the younger population in the past two years.

Faculty in a variety of disciplines use blogging software in their courses. The most common purposes for such blogs include communication and interaction between the professor and the students, communication and interaction between the students, requiring students to engage in online writing as a means of teaching them the genre and what it means to make one's thinking visible, teaching students to work with online materials in a critical way, and introducing them to what it means to be part of a community of practice.[27] These lofty instructional goals are only rarely realized when the pixels meet the road. Unless the reasons for asking/requiring writing in a class blog are made very clear, too often students will see the blog as just one more assignment to complete. This instrumental approach to the requirements of a course results in situations where professors must require X number of postings in the blog over the course of the semester, and Y number of comments on other posts; otherwise, very little of substance actually happens on a class blog. A second reason that student blogging only rarely lives up to its potential is that there is often little concrete payoff for the students, other than completing a requirement in the syllabus. What do they get from their online writing other than a grade? Do their blog posts show up somewhere else as well? Are others, outside the classroom, connecting with them through their blog posts? Because the answers to these questions are most often "no," most class blogs go silent the minute the semester ends. That class blogs die at the end of the semester should be no surprise, because students so rarely see any benefit to a class blog beyond the grade they earn in that class.

A different approach—one that helps students see blogging as being more relevant to their lives as students, citizens, and humans, and that takes advantage of the fact that they already spend a great deal of time as creators of online content—can yield better, or at least more long-term, results. If, instead of contributing posts to a class blog that goes up at the beginning of the semester and dies at the end, students are required to create their own personal blog that they can use for any number of purposes—not just class assignments—then instructors tend to see a much higher level of engagement in the online writing process. The vast majority of students already have some sort of online identity when they walk into our classrooms. If the blogging they do for a class supplements that preexisting identity, they are much more likely to invest the time and effort we expect from them, and we can stop requiring them to participate in the class blog a certain number of times each week. Some may choose to simply feed what they write on a personal blog onto their other online presences (Facebook, Tumblr, etc.). Others may establish more formal presences online as historians.[28] With an RSS feed, their contributions to their own personal blogs can then be fed automatically into a class blog that aggregates what the students are writing in their own writing spaces. As my colleague Dan Cohen writes in the syllabus to his graduate course, Clio Wired, students are expected to "think of this class not as meeting once a week but as an ongoing conversation that is active all semester."[29] If students set up an RSS feed to aggregate content from the blog they create as history students into their other web presences—Facebook, a personal website, and so on—that is a clear sign they are seeing their class work as part of who they are online. As a result, they begin to write more carefully (because what they write shows up elsewhere in their digital lives, not just on a class page), and often with more energy and enthusiasm. We already know that a significant share of students—perhaps as many as one-third according to a recent EDUCAUSE survey—write in a blog as part of their daily lives, so asking them to do so as part of their educational lives is not much of a stretch.[30]

Teachers who assign this sort of online writing have to make a number of decisions about the rules of the game. In a class blog where all students contribute to something created by the professor, it is much easier to set strict rules for such things as tone (formal vs. casual), attention to the rules of grammar, syntax, and spelling/capitalization, what can and cannot be embedded in a blog post, and so on. But when students are creating their own blogs/microblogs, these are their writing and self-presentation spaces and so if the rules of the course are too strict, it is reasonable to assume that their engagement with the assignment to do online writing for their history class will be less than it might otherwise be.[31] This is not to say that instructors should waive all rules when it comes to the work students submit from their blogs to a class blog. However, it is well worth considering what sort of leeway students can reasonably be granted in the service of generating broader engagement with, and active commitment to, the work of a class. Among the most important reasons for granting students greater freedom with their online writing spaces that are used for a class is that they take much greater ownership of the content when it is part of their online presence, rather than merely something they submit to a professor's online space. When they begin to take that level of ownership of their work, students often produce much more insightful work and/or pay closer attention to such things as grammar and syntax (which historians care about as well as the level of historical analysis). If instructors are going to give students the freedom to write about and make history as they choose in their own online spaces, then it is incumbent on the professor to step back as far as he or she is willing to go and let students do what they think needs to be done, even if that means stretching as far as possible the limits an instructor places on the assignments for the course.

Wikis

When I began writing my own blog in the fall of 2005, one of the first issues I addressed was what history teachers should make of the growing ubiquity of *Wikipedia* in the work students were submitting.[32] Already in 2005, *Wikipedia* was becoming the "go-to" source for history students, especially because students using any one of the major Internet search engines to find information on a historical topic not only typically found a *Wikipedia* entry at or near the top of the search returns, but also found that same information repeated in numerous other websites that draw their content directly from *Wikipedia*. If a half dozen websites cite the same information, then it must be correct—at least in the eyes of the casual or inexperienced user. The initial impulse of many history teachers was to warn their students off *Wikipedia* at all costs, and some even banned the use of *Wikipedia* altogether.[33] Telling students they may not use an information resource rarely has much of an impact, and so history teachers have little choice but to either (a) ignore the problem in the hope that it will go away, or (b) embrace the *Wikipedia* phenomenon as a teaching opportunity. After all, we do not want students to think that relying on encyclopedias—any sort of encyclopedia—is the right way to do historical research, so using *Wikipedia* as a tool to impart lessons about the strengths and weaknesses of encyclopedias can work very well. If the lessons students learn are hands-on, meaning they involve the actual manipulation of content on *Wikipedia,* then we are teaching them something else as well—how to work with wikis in all their complexity and variety.[34]

How then might one best approach teaching students to work appropriately with *Wikipedia?* The simple answer is to have them write their own entries for the encyclopedia, or to substantially edit an existing entry that needs expanding. Although the editing syntax in *Wikipedia* is not particularly intuitive, it is clearly easy enough to use, given the hundreds of thousands (if not millions) of people who have created and edited entries there. Because so many others have figured out how to work with *Wikipedia's* editing system, I provide my students with almost no training whatsoever. I simply point out that there is an "edit" tab on every entry in their favorite encyclopedia, then show them what the edit window looks like, and then I make a simple editorial correction to an entry so they can see how it is done. Then I leave it to them to figure out the rest. Before turning them loose on *Wikipedia,* however, I also engage them in a discussion of some of the most important epistemological issues related to encyclopedia writing. What does it mean to write something with a "neutral point of view"? Can history really be without bias, as *Wikipedia's* editorial policies require? What does it mean to have a bias and how would we recognize it. Why would *Wikipedia* have an injunction against original research? What do they think of *Wikipedia's* standard—verifiability, not truth? What makes a subject sufficiently "notable" to be included in the world's largest encyclopedia?[35] What does it mean for historians to try to write in these ways under these restrictions?[36]

In addition to helping students begin to grapple with some of the thorny issues that encyclopedias raise, asking them to write for *Wikipedia* helps them to understand what it means to create history that is malleable, that can be changed by anyone at any time. What does it mean to have historical information crowdsourced? Can the collective wisdom of the crowd be reasonably compared to the wisdom of a scholar who has devoted years to the study of a particular historical topic? When this latter question is asked in that way, students typically agree that scholars with deep knowledge of a subject are generally to be trusted over the wisdom of the crowd. But then, if the context is changed and these same students are asked if a music critic with decades of experience listening to and writing about popular music should be trusted over tens of thousands of people who bought a song because they liked it, the question of crowdsourcing becomes a little less clear to them. As my colleague Roy Rosenzweig asked in 2006, can history really be open source?[37] Once students begin to confront some of the central issues related to this question, writing for *Wikipedia* turns out to be an intellectually challenging task.

A second advantage of asking them to write for *Wikipedia,* or in any wiki space, is that wiki writing is so easily collaborative. A third is that the inherent malleability of wikis forces students to think about the various ways knowledge can be organized in a digital space.[38] Wikis permit the organization of information in a whole variety of ways—the structure chosen by *Wikipedia* is but one of many. When students are asked how their work ought to be organized and are shown examples of various forms of possible organization, they are forced back on Michael Wesch's point about form and content being separable in the Web 2.0 world. Data—in the form of text, images, video, or sounds—can be stored in wikis in various ways and then presented online in a form the student or students select. If the text created in a class wiki is one that all students have access to, then that text can be written, rewritten, and rewritten again until some consensus is reached about what, exactly, it ought to say and how that ought to be said. In this way, students can take part in an ongoing conversation about the construction of historical knowledge—much as professional historians do, but within the space of a wiki.[39] Finally, the fact that wikis retain all versions of a particular text introduces students to the possibility of historical research that can be conducted on something they or someone else has written. How does the revision history reflect changing attitudes about a particular subject? What does it mean to reach consensus in a public space like a wiki? Are there "better" and "worse" versions of knowledge in a wiki that ought to be highlighted by historians? These are all historians' questions, and asking students to grapple with them as they create historical knowledge online has many advantages. By forcing them to actively engage in public knowledge production—to help make history in the world's most popular information resource—we can give them both an opportunity to be historians, if only for a brief moment, and to assume public ownership of their own work products.

To help my students get started with *Wikipedia* I tell them about my own first experiences as an editor of an entry in the encyclopedia. In April 2006, I read a story in the *New Yorker* about new work by historical archaeologists that cast some doubt on the claims that the Donner family had resorted to cannibalism to survive being snowbound in the Sierra Nevada Mountains. Because *Wikipedia* had recently become a resource I was seeing students use more and more often, I thought I would see what the Donner Party entry had to say on this subject. The version I found read:

> The Donner Party was a group of California-bound American settlers caught up in the "westering fever" of the 1840s. After becoming snowbound in the Sierra Nevada mountains in the winter of 1846–1847, some of the emigrants resorted to cannibalism.[40]

I created an account, and then edited the entry.

> The Donner Party was a group of California-bound American settlers caught up in the "westering fever" of the 1840s. Accounts of the Donner Party's journey traditionally claim that after becoming snowbound in the Sierra Nevada mountains in the winter of 1846–1847, some of the emigrants resorted to cannibalism, but recent research by historical archeologists now casts doubt on this part of the story.[41]

That version of the opening paragraph lasted for five days, at which point someone changed it.

> The Donner Party was a group of California-bound American settlers caught up in the "westering fever" of the 1840s. After becoming snowbound in the Sierra Nevada mountains in the winter of 1846–1847, some of the emigrants resorted to cannibalism, although this aspect of the tragedy has been exaggerated.[42]

Since my original editing of the Donner Party entry in 2008, that entry has been edited more than 3,000 times by an uncounted number of users. On June 30, 2011, the opening paragraph read:

The Donner Party (sometimes called the Donner–Reed Party) was a group of American pioneers who set out for California in a wagon train. Delayed by a series of mishaps, they spent the winter of 1846–47 snowbound in the Sierra Nevada. Some of the emigrants resorted to cannibalism to survive, eating those who had succumbed to starvation and sickness.[43]

I ask my students to work their way through the history of this entry, picking random moments in that chronology to access versions of the entry to see how the opening paragraph has changed over time. This exercise introduces them, in a simple way, to some of the most important issues of crowdsourced information. It also gives me a chance to discuss how entries in wikis, whether *Wikipedia* or any other wiki they might use, represent a series of compromises by a community of people interested in that particular entry. The June 2011 version of the Donner Party entry is not that different from the revisions I made more than three years earlier, but there is an important difference with the entry I found when I went to the page for the first time. In that version, the opening paragraph simply said, "some of the emigrants resorted to cannibalism." Over the years, a slightly more nuanced version of that simple statement has evolved from constant editing and reediting of this entry by the community of people interested in how the Donner Party is portrayed in *Wikipedia*. What has almost disappeared, however, is the information I added about the work of forensic archaeologists. In the version of the entry I examined on December 1, 2011, the only reference to their work is a sentence, far down in the entry, that reads, "Archaeological findings at the Alder Creek camp proved inconclusive for evidence of cannibalism," followed by a reference to a more recent book on the party.[44] Seeing how quickly my addition of a reference to work by scholars, work that challenged popular notions of the history of the party, disappeared from the entry helps students see both how malleable such entries are, but also how an anti-research bias often finds its way into *Wikipedia* entries. The point of this exercise is not to convince students that *Wikipedia* is somehow "bad," but rather to teach them about the ways historical knowledge is created in public spaces.

Over the years, my students have almost all enjoyed writing entries for *Wikipedia,* and several have become very active in the *Wikipedia* editorial community, taking ownership of various entries. Being part of this larger community of writers and editors not only gives the students a clear sense for just how malleable information in their favorite encyclopedia can be, but also introduces them to being part of a community of historical practice, even if only in a very small way. They are often quite offended when someone changes something they have written in an entry, and are even more unhappy if one of the *Wikipedia* editing bots deletes something they have written for being insufficiently notable. Others are thrilled when "their" entry catches the attention of other readers, and people out there in the wilds of the Internet begin to change and improve what they have written. For example, in February 2007, one of my students wrote an entry on David and Catherine Birnie of Australia, the only known husband and wife serial killers.[45] I did not really want to know why she was interested in the Birnies, but it was something she wanted to write about, and she did well. By the end of the semester, her entry had been edited many times by others, and she was quite proud of the form it had taken by May of that year. That particular student has gone on to become an active *Wikipedia* editor, and continues to work on various entries that she has an interest in or commitment to. Her experiences demonstrate the value of giving students assignments that require them to take active roles in the making of history online.

This final example speaks to a theme woven throughout this book— the need to engage students where they live—namely, in the digital space where they are creating content for others to see, use, and remix. The malleability of information is a notion that students are often much more comfortable with than we generally are. Our teaching strategies need to change to help them explore new ways to combine what they do daily— create online content—with what we do. By showing them how the practices of the professional historian can be adapted to the digital realm, we help them see the process of online content creation as something more than just fun or "what they do." Instead, it becomes a way to *be* historians in the digital space, to analyze historical information, and then present it in ways that are useful to others, that have staying power well beyond the end of the semester and the awarding of a grade, and that have relevance to the lives they are living now and plan to live after graduation.

< 5 >

Making

DIY History?

I have used it long enough to observe that students don't benefit from the use of many types of technology.

—Anonymous respondent to a survey by the American Historical Association, 2010[1]

But mine's better.

—Undergraduate history student at George Mason University[2]

A 2010 survey by Robert Townsend of the American Historical Association makes it abundantly clear that historians teaching at American colleges and universities remain profoundly skeptical of the value of using digital media to teach their students about the past. Although wide majorities of those teaching undergraduates have adopted slideware such as PowerPoint to display images or outlines on a screen, only a tiny fraction use any of the new digital platforms that offer users the opportunity to engage one another or to generate their own online content (blogs, wikis, social-networking platforms like Facebook or Twitter).[3] Only slightly more than half of those responding to Townsend's survey indicated that they use any online sources in their undergraduate courses. These findings stand in stark contrast to what we know about how students seek out and work with historical content—online sources are almost always their first (and perhaps even second and third) choice before turning to more traditional media like printed sources. Townsend's findings also stand in stark contrast

102

to historians' use of digital media in their own work. Almost 70 percent of the more than 4,000 historians responding to his survey say they regularly use online sources. The disconnect between historians' attitudes about their own use of online content and their students' use of content in that same medium is surprising at best, shocking at worst.

But the problem goes deeper than this disconnect. It is not just that those teaching history courses at American colleges and universities to undergraduates discourage their students from doing what they themselves do. Those same historians are watching from the dock as the ship called Web 2.0 sails away, carrying our students off to a distant shore that we almost never visit. Surveys of American young people, such as those conducted by the Pew Research Center, demonstrate just how actively the students in our classrooms participate in the Web 2.0 world that is all about connections between users (social networks), users creating content instead of passively consuming content, and users bending the technology to their own needs.[4] Townsend's data indicate that fewer than 10 percent of faculty teaching undergraduate history courses in the United States use Web 2.0 media such as blogs, Twitter, wikis, or Facebook, or other social-networking platforms in their classes. The data cited earlier (from the Pew Internet project) indicate that more than 75 percent of all Americans between the ages of 18 and 29 have created one or more profiles on a social-networking site, and that while only 14 percent have used Twitter, this age group represents the most active among Twitter users.[5] As these two very different surveys indicate, history teachers are using technology to teach their students about the past in ways that are very far removed from the reality of students' lives—at least the technologically mediated aspects of those lives. We already know that students are voting with their feet when it comes to using or not using digital media—and they are voting in favor of the digital world despite any disinclination their professors might show.

In addition to the fact that students are much more avid users of digital media for learning than we might prefer, historians need to consider the many ways that students are beginning to use those media to create new and often quite different forms of history. I have already described the newsreel that one of my undergraduate students "fixed" for me in a Western Civilization class half a decade ago, and how that student's work seemed to me to be a precursor of an emerging sensibility about the malleability of historical content among undergraduate students. It is worth remembering that students live in a remix culture—where popular music, film, and fiction all draw on multiple sources—many of them created by other authors, directors, or musicians, and repackage that content in new ways to create cultural artifacts that often have large audiences. It is from this culture that we get media such as Sophia Coppola's 2006 film *Marie Antoinette* (2006), which combined such historical moments as a masquerade ball in prerevolutionary Versailles with a soundtrack featuring Souixsie and the Banshees, novels such as Seth Grahame-Smith's *Abraham Lincoln: Vampire Hunter,* and Ben H. Winters's literary mash-up, *Sense and Sensibility and Sea Monsters.*[6] While historians might be tempted to scoff at such mash-ups and remixes as ahistorical or simply silly, the popularity of such work cannot be denied. Grahame-Smith's Lincoln novel debuted at number four on the *New York Times* best-seller list and has been made into a feature film. Film remixes of the past have been around for as long as feature films have existed. As Princeton University's Natalie Zemon-Davis has argued, historical feature films are better seen as "thought experiments," rather than necessarily historically accurate, and so should be judged by a different set of standards than historical accuracy.[7] After all, as Davis points out, historians have a long history of using "made up, but appropriate speeches" by prominent historical figures.[8] Only in the past several centuries has this practice fallen out of favor. How many students of the ancient world have read Pericles's oration after the battle of Marathon without having any idea that this speech—considered by many to be one of the great moments in Western oratory—was Thucydides's imaginative mash-up of what he imagined Pericles might have, or should have, said?[9]

Already, we are seeing signs—more than just the "fixed" newsreel that my student brought to my Western Civilization class—that historians and their students are creating new and different ways to represent their research about the past. For instance, Canadian educator Neil Stephenson has created something called the "Cigar Box Project," in which his grade-seven students tell the story of Canadian history with cigar box panels they create in digital media (eventually building their own boxes). The mash-ups of Canadian history they create are rooted in notions of the past that any historian would understand and approve of, but also reveal a playful sensibility about design, historical presentation, and originality that might make many history teachers uncomfortable.[10] Similarly, the popular video-sharing and social-networking website YouTube is filled with remixes of historical video. To cite but one example, a fruitful hour could be spent examining all the ways the story of the "Tank Man" of Tiananmen Square in 1989 is being told on YouTube. You can watch American television news footage of his courageous act of standing in front of a line of tanks (an original source of sorts). One can watch Chinese state news footage of this same event (the same video, but a very a different version of the narrative of his actions), or one can watch remixes of those broadcasts with entirely new audio tracks—everything from classical piano to rock and roll. Perhaps the most interesting version currently available is one that mashes up the now-iconic footage of the Tank Man facing down a line of tanks with a speech by the American student activist Mario Savio on the steps of Sproul Hall at the University of California, Berkeley, on December 2, 1964. As we watch the events in China, we hear Savio speaking.

> . . . and in time when the operation of the machine becomes so odious, makes you so sick at heart, that you can't take part, that you can't even passively take part. And you've got to put your body upon the gears, upon the wheels, upon the levers, upon all the apparatus, and you've got to make it stop, and you've got to indicate to the people who run it, to the people around it, that unless you're free, the machine will be prevented from working at all . . .[11]

This particular version of the Tank Man story is "Little Man vs. Big Machine," and is set to Boards of Canada's "Music is Math"—a far cry from the audio tracks of CNN or Chinese state television. Since this particular version of the Tank Man video appeared on YouTube it has had more than 360,000 views (as of January 1, 2012). How many historians of the events of 1989 in China can claim an audience of that size? Moreover, this video remix of the Tank Man's exploits is just one of dozens of remixes of that same short video clip—everything from a short clip on how to dance the "Tank Man Tango," to a serious eight-part documentary film on Tiananmen Square and the Tank Man's role in it. Each of these is an authentic, if not original, representation of those events—in their own way "thought experiments," to use Natalie Zemon Davis's way of describing what filmmakers do when they make history on film.[12] My own student's remix of that Nuremberg video was of a piece with these other thought experiments. Lest you doubt the power of video sharing websites such as YouTube, according to Michael Wesch, since 1948 the three major American television networks (ABC, NBC, CBS) have delivered approximately 1.5 million hours of programming over the airwaves, while YouTube users uploaded more than that in the first six months of 2008.[13]

Of course, the majority of what is uploaded to YouTube is not what we might call quality programming, but somewhere in the 9,000-plus hours of video uploaded to the website each day, some of that material is of a quality equal to or better than what appears on the legacy networks—and almost all of that content is created not by studios, but by individuals. While historical video would not make any Top Ten list of tomorrow's uploads, the thousands, if not tens of thousands, of historical videos— remixes and original versions—attest to the power of this medium to shape students' understanding of the past. Among the more popular historical video channels on YouTube at the moment when I wrote the final draft of this book was "Music for History Lovers," the creation of high school history teachers Amy Burvall and Herb Mahelona. Burvall and Mahelona have converted the history of Western Civilization into a series of MTV-like music videos that combine a very playful sensibility with a serious teaching purpose. Between April 2008 and December 2011 their YouTube channel had registered more than 4.2 million views of videos ranging from the history of the Trojan Wars set to a song by Culture Club, to a history of the French Revolution set to a song by Lady Gaga. As Burvall and Mahelona explain in a TED talk in November 2011, their work includes a significant amount of collaboration with their students—everything from photography to lyrics—and that by opening their work to a global audience through digital media, that work has been transformed by feedback received from their increasingly huge audience.[14] At least in the realm of digital video, we have already reached the stage where Carl Becker's Mr. Everyman has indeed become his own historian.

What is a historian to do when faced by this emerging sensibility about a malleable past? One option is to ignore it, deny its existence, or simply forbid students to have anything to do with it, as the members of Middlebury College's department of history did several years ago when they banned the use of *Wikipedia* in their courses.[15] The other option is to take a more forward approach to teaching students about the past and at least make an attempt to meet them where they live. Instead of assuming that "students don't benefit from the use of many types of technology" as the anonymous professor quoted at the outset of this chapter believes, we should do our best to teach them how to make the most of digital media by taking advantage of their creative impulses. We need to give them room to create, even as we teach them to think like historians.[16] What follows is one example of how I have approached the challenges posed by students' views of how the past can, or should, be used, analyzed, and presented. The course described below evolved from several years of thinking about how best to address both the pervasive problem of students' lack of skepticism about sources—online or analog—and their interest in creating content for the Internet, rather than merely consuming it and regurgitating what they consumed in a five-, seven-, or ten-page paper. I also wanted my students to have some fun while they were confronting real historical issues. The results of this teaching experiment have not been without controversy. More than a few historians and librarians (and even someone posting on my blog under the name Jimmy Wales—the founder of *Wikipedia*) were not amused. I have been called "pond scum," "sociopathic," and even received one death threat after a writer for the Atlantic.com wrote a story about the second iteration of the course.[17] Others found the exercise thought provoking and worthy of deeper consideration. *Wikipedia* editors had an energetic debate about what to do about the way my students decided to use *Wikipedia* in their projects—a debate that offers some very interesting insights into the thinking processes and community standards of the world's largest encyclopedia.[18] The point I would like to make with this example is not that it should be emulated in the specific, but rather, in the general sense, by which I mean it demonstrates the power of meeting students where they live in the digital world. If they make history using digital media, they are much more likely to understand history, and to embrace it as more than just a subject they are interested in. They will become historians themselves, some of them in ways we have not yet thought of.

Lying About the Past and the Last American Pirate

I have already described one rewrite of the historical methods course—Dead in Virginia—in which my students wrote extensively in a class database. An earlier rewrite of the methods course was called Lying About the Past. In this version of the course, I jettisoned all emphasis on historiography in favor of a focus on creating historical content in digital media in an attempt to teach a course focused on making and creating content, rather than learning about the works of the great historians. Also, because I had already seen evidence of students (and the public at large) taking a more playful approach to the past, I decided to access my own sense of fun to see what we might accomplish when we combined serious historical work with a playful sensibility. I wanted my students to have fun, while learning serious things.

My willingness to let my students play around with the past is not without precedent. Carl Becker shows this in his 1931 essay "Everyman His Own Historian."

> Mr. Everyman works with something of the freedom of a creative artist; the history which he imaginatively recreates as an artificial extension of his personal experience will inevitably be an engaging blend of fact and fancy, a mythical adaptation of that which actually happened. In part it will be true, in part false; as a whole perhaps neither true nor false, but only the most convenient form of error. Not that Mr. Everyman wishes or intends to deceive himself or others.[19]

Almost two millennia before Becker, Thucydides explained his approach to recording the great speeches of his day.

> With reference to the speeches in this history, some were delivered before the war began, others while it was going on; some I heard myself, others I got from various quarters; it was in all cases difficult to carry them word for word in one's memory, so my habit has been to make the speakers say what was in my opinion demanded of them by the various occasions, of course adhering as closely as possible to the general sense of what they really said.[20]

Fortified by such quotations from two of the lions of the historiography (along with all of their colleagues) I dropped from my course, I rewrote my methods course. There are many ways one could approach a revision of the historical methods course. The approach I settled on for this rewrite of the course might best be called "slash and burn." While I retained some of the core teaching practices, including group work, problem-based learning, and what I thought were some fairly innovative in- and out-of-class exercises, I junked the rest of the syllabus and started over, using the Wiggina/McTighe version of backwards design.

My decision to redesign the course around a playful approach to the past arose from two sources. Over the years I have become convinced that history as a discipline has become a bit too stodgy for its own good. It seems to me that we are taking ourselves a little too seriously of late (if there was ever a time when we did not). The second source for my decision to try to be more playful was an experience I had teaching a large group of fifth-grade students about historical research. While some might be tempted to argue that elementary students cannot do sophisticated historical research, I am in the Bruce VanSledright camp and believe that fifth graders can do some very good historical work when given the proper tools and context.[21] During the hour and a half I had with approximately seventy-five fifth-grade students, I not only found that they could work with primary sources such as military service records from the Civil War and pages from the U.S. Census, I also noticed how much fun they had while doing it—fun I do not see my own students having when I give them similarly complex sources to work with. For instance, when it was time for them to start writing, those fifth graders threw themselves down on the floor, self-organized into groups, and started drawing pictures to go with what they were writing. They laughed, they chatted, they made faces as they concentrated. In short, they were kinetic, engaged, and as focused as eleven-year-olds get. And they produced some really good history from the sources I gave them.[22] What happens to young people, I wondered, between the fifth grade and university to convince them that historical research is not fun? Is it them? Or is it the course? Or is it me? I am almost never willing to blame the shortcomings of a course on the students taking the course, and am confident enough in my abilities as an instructor to not blame myself (too much), so I decided that it was a combination of the course and my approach to the course that was to blame.[23] Part of my goal in the design of a new version of the methods course was to recapture the sense of fun that those eleven-year-olds demonstrated when they were doing their historical research.

When I began rewriting my syllabus, I tried hard to retain as much of what I had seen during my day with that group of fifth graders. The course I created, Lying About the Past, was organized around an exploration of historical hoaxes. In the first half of the semester the students did what students do in most history classes—they read books and articles, watched documentaries, discussed these materials both in small groups and as a class operating in seminar mode, and they even wrote two five-page papers analyzing information gleaned from the materials I assigned. The reading list, however, was fairly unconventional for an upper-level history course. The first article we read was "The Violence of the Lambs" by John Jeremiah Sullivan, which appeared in the February 2008 issue of that stodgy academic journal *GQ* (*Gentleman's Quarterly*).[24] This article, a hoax that ends with a brief paragraph in which Sullivan admits to making up most of the story—an admission he says he did not want to make but that his editor insisted upon—signaled to the students that mine was not your typical history course.

I also told them, on day one, via the syllabus, just how I felt about history and fun in the context of the course they were signed up for.

> I believe that the study of history ought to be fun and that too often historians (I include myself in this category) take an overly stuffy approach to the past. Maybe it's our conditioning in graduate school, or maybe we're afraid that if we get too playful with our field we won't be taken seriously as scholars. Whatever the reason, I think history has just gotten a bit too boring for its own good. This course is my attempt to lighten up a little and see where it gets us.[25]

Not surprisingly, the seventeen undergraduates in the first iteration of the course and the thirty-plus in the second iteration took to my approach to the course with gusto. There is not a single "serious" academic work on the syllabus—no Herodotus, no Thucydides, no von Ranke, no Foucault, and no Nora. Instead, we read works by popularizers you have probably never heard of, watched documentaries such as *Český sen* (*Czech Dream*) and faux documentaries like *The Old Negro Space Program,* and searched websites such as the Museum of Hoaxes and Snopes.com for useful information about historical hoaxes.[26] In eighteen years of college teaching I do not think I have ever had a group of students be as consistently prepared for class as these two groups of students, or think so critically as a group about the fundamental principles of historical research and scholarship, and what it means when the public engages with the results of historical scholarship. Both times I taught the class my students worked *hard.*

Up to the midpoint of the semester nothing we do in Lying About the Past is particularly controversial. I am sure that plenty of colleagues around the country might look a bit askance at the "soft" readings I assign, but at least my students are doing research and writing papers. These papers all included the kind of research skills that a history course is intended to teach them, including identifying a topic, creating a thesis they can support with evidence gleaned from research, then finding an appropriate set of primary and secondary sources to support their argument. All of these assignments will be familiar to anyone who teaches historical methods. It is instead what happens in the second half of the course that is unusual, generative, and that turns out to be a bit controversial.

After the seventh week of the semester my students began building their own historical hoax, a hoax they eventually launched into the digital world with great pride and satisfaction, not to mention a fair amount of glee. Using a consensus model, I asked everyone to come up with ideas for a possible hoax, and as a class they winnowed the choices down to two finalists. The students developed the standards for what the hoax should be, including that it would have to be historical, that it would have to be plausible to fool people who encountered it, that there would be a sufficient evidentiary basis for that plausibility, and that there would be a "hoaxable community" out there (i.e., a community of people liable to buy into the hoax because it appealed to them for personal or professional reasons). The first time I taught the course, to their surprise (and mine) the hoaxable community turned out to be one the students did not expect—academic historians and educational technologists. The second time I taught the course, the students were less successful as hoaxers, but their attempts generated much more media and public interest.[27]

The hoax the first class finally settled on—The Last American Pirate— was organized around the senior research project of a fictitious student the class named Jane Browning (a name chosen because it was so common), who uncovered her Virginia pirate quite by accident. This man, Edward Owens, was a Confederate veteran who, during the Long Depression that began in 1873, found that he could no longer support his family by oyster fishing and so turned briefly to a life of sea-borne crime. He and his crew of two robbed pleasure boaters in the Lower Chesapeake until the economy recovered, at which point Owens went back to fishing and clean living. He left behind a legend and, as luck would have it, a last will and testament detailing both his exploits and his guilt over what he had done. There really was a man named Edward Owens who lived along the Lower Chesapeake at the time, and my students chose his name for two reasons—he really did exist, and they could find no evidence that any of the millions of genealogists out there knew anything about the real Edward Owens.[28] Also, the name Edward Owens was generic enough that a Google search would turn up too many possibilities to be sorted through in a timely manner. The platform the students chose for perpetrating their hoax was one they were very familiar with—a blog assigned by "Jane's" professor as part of a senior research seminar (Jane was a history major at an unnamed university).[29] Along the way, Jane chronicled her search for a topic, her search for sources, her attempts to make sense of what she found, and finally her struggles with writing up the results of her work. In addition to the blog, she posted several YouTube videos, posted notices in social-networking sites such as Stumbleon.com, and created an entry on Edward Owens in *Wikipedia*.[30] Before deciding on a student blog as the best way to perpetrate their hoax, the students also discussed creating a website, but in the end decided it would be too much trouble. As we will see, the choice of a student blog had important implications for who ended up falling victim to the hoax.

At the beginning of the semester I tell the students that their hoax can run until the last day of class, at which point we will expose it ourselves (if someone had not found us out already). I think it is fair to say that each time I've taught the course the majority of the students, if not all, would have preferred to let the hoax live on until it was exposed by someone in the wider world, but I insist that we shut it down at the end of the term. Had the students not exposed their hoax it is an open question how long Edward Owens or the "beer of 1812" might have survived online. For one thing, my students always choose innocuous hoaxes, so the question of who the "last" American pirate was is not one that attracts a great deal of attention. Even with the publicity that accrued from the post-exposure controversy, as of April 30, 2010, only 7,500 unique visitors had been to Jane's website. A primary reason why the students chose a pirate hoax was because they thought the pirate lovers of the world—especially those who enjoy International Talk Like a Pirate Day—represented a hoaxable audience. When the fall of 2008 turned out to be a period of intense media interest in piracy because of the activities of real pirates off the coast of Somalia, my students thought they had stumbled into the perfect topic for their hoax. Alas, those with "piratitude" failed to take notice of Edward Owens until after the hoax was exposed.[31] Instead, much to the student's satisfaction, history teachers were the ones taken in by the false pirate and his student historian.

Only a few days after the hoax appeared online, academic bloggers—including history teachers and professors, instructional technologists, and librarians—began writing about Jane's blog as an exemplar of how undergraduate students could use new media to represent their research and writing in digital form.[32] The hoax found its way into the academic blogosphere because two graduate students at my university's Center for History and New Media tweeted about it on their personal Twitter feeds—not as a hoax, but as evidence of an interesting research result from an undergraduate student: "This is incredible: A history student has found the last American pirate."[33] These two tweets found their way through the Twitterverse to several academic bloggers who then wrote about Jane's project on their own blogs. It is worth quoting one at length to provide a sense for how Jane and her project was embraced by academics enthusiastic for digital media.

> I found not only a really cool example of the power of these tools for an individual to track and frame their own educational experience, but some absolutely exciting research about a 19th century Pirate (possibly the last US pirate of his kind) no one's ever heard of: Edward Owens. This undergraduate took her research to the next level by framing the experience on her blog, full with images and details from her Library of Congress research, video interviews with scholars and her visit to Owens [*sic*] house, her bibliography, along with a link to the *Wikipedia* page she created for this little known local pirate.

> What's even cooler is the fact that she not only framed a digital space for her research by getting her own domain and setting up a blog there, but she understood that she could also protect her identity at the same time by keeping certain information private. It is such a perfect example of the importance of framing your identity as a student/scholar online, and it really buttresses beautifully with the ideas we've been thinking about recently in regards to digital identity at UMW. More than that though, is the fact that this project was hers and she was fired up about what she had accomplished, and she could actually share that fact with others through her blog.[34]

Academic victims also interacted with Jane directly, writing comments on her blog such as, "What you have done here in documenting your experience is an amazing example of the power of technology in aiding historical research. Well done."[35] That academics turned out to be the primary victims of the hoax generated some controversy in the academic blogosphere—a controversy discussed in more detail below. In the aftermath of the hoax's exposure the class received some media exposure and then, like all small stories, this one died away.[36]

In the spring 2012 semester, students in a second iteration of this course created two hoaxes—one revolving around a beer recipe from 1812 and another about a man who might have been a serial killer in New York City in 1897. Neither of these was as successful as the last American pirate hoax.

What then did my students learn from playing with the past in this way?

Historians are fond of saying that one of our main goals in teaching is that students should learn to "think historically." As seen in chapter 1, the list of characteristics and abilities that fall under the heading of historical thinking can be quite broad, but that there is an important distinction between content knowledge and procedural knowledge. Because I essentially dispense with historiography in this course in favor of letting my students quite literally "make history," it is the latter that my course emphasizes. To be sure, students in the first iteration of the course learned some things about nineteenth-century Virginia history and about maritime history in general, while those in the second iteration learned about the brewery industry, the war of 1812, and New York City at the turn of the previous century, but this content was incidental to the larger lessons about methods. First and foremost my students had to understand how knowledge is constructed in the digital realm, but also in the analog world. Their goal was to create a narrative built on enough "true facts" that the "false facts" would go unnoticed. To do that, they had to acquire a fairly sophisticated understanding of how such historical knowledge is created online and the digital skills necessary to make that happen. But to acquire the "true facts" they needed to make the "false facts" plausible—they needed to know how to find the information they needed on such things as the maritime history of the lower Chesapeake or the war of 1812. When we teach historical methods to students, one of the goals we generally espouse is teaching students to do research in places other than the web. Much of what my students used for their hoaxes—the "true facts"—came from libraries and archives rather than websites, in part because the sources they needed just are not online. For me this was a very positive result of the course, but one that was largely coincidental to the topics they selected.

More important to my learning goals was teaching my students to be much more critical consumers of online content. As discussed in chapter 2, too often these days students search for plausible information using the "type some keywords into Google and see what comes up" method. When a reasonable source appears through such a search, they often use that source with almost no critical analysis of the quality of that source.[37] In other words, they spend little or no time "adjudicat[ing] between competing versions (and visions) of the past."[38] Instead, they seem to employ a rough and ready plausibility test: "Does it look good enough? Okay then, I'll use it." In contrast to this attitude about finding and using plausible information, one of the students in the first version of the class recently wrote a comment in my blog as a response to an earlier essay I wrote on the course.

> I guess what I am trying to say in a very long winded and wordy sort of way is that we as historians, in this day and age of technology, should know better than to take anything anyone sends us at face value, I don't care if someone tweeted about it, or if they updated their status on facebook. Not because everyone is out there to deceive us, but because in a day and age of technology it is so easy to create a story or an idea and cover your tracks.[39]

The students who took this class will almost surely think twice before ever employing such a plausibility test with content they find online and, one hopes, historical content in any form, given the amount of time we spent discussing the prevalence of what a colleague calls "zombie facts" in the historical literature. For instance, we devoted close to half a class period examining just how ubiquitous and tenacious H. L. Mencken's fabricated story about the first bathtub in the White House has turned out to be.[40] The profound skepticism my students acquire in this course will serve them well throughout the rest of their lives, not merely in their work as historians. That this skepticism has value beyond the history curriculum was highlighted in a comment on the course by Bill Smith of the University of Arkansas, who wrote that in a world where many believe that the Moon landing was a fake, "A healthy skepticism is an important part of citizenship."[41]

One of the things historians often spend a lot of time on in their courses is the nature of historical sources—which are primary sources, which are secondary sources, what sorts of tests should be applied to each category (primary, secondary) and each type within that category (text, image, film, artifact), and each subtype (text: novel, letter, government report, newspaper story, poem, sacred text)? Because my students had to create at least a few invented sources to set beside real sources from archives and libraries, they needed to think carefully and critically about the nature of each type of source, if only so we would know better how to fake them. One type of source that historians have devoted a lot of ink and many pixels to is photographic images. Students often like to think of photographs as being particularly authentic representations of reality at the moment the photographer snapped the picture. After all, the camera does not lie, does it?[42] In this age of Photoshop and digital-image manipulation, many students are at least a little skeptical about some images, and the obvious cases like the "Bert is Evil" website are easy for them to figure out.[43] But what about more sophisticated fakery like the amazing disappearing Trotsky, in which Soviet publicists were required to excise Trotsky from all publications in the Soviet Union after he and Stalin had their falling out?[44] The manipulation of images my students engaged in for the pirate and serial killer hoaxes was not nearly up to Soviet standards. They merely made images too small to read so the reader of Jane's blog could not see them clearly enough, or clipped out passages from a nineteenth-century will to support a particular version of the story they wanted blog readers to see.[45] But they did learn how easy it is to lie with an image, and so came away from the course as skeptical not only of text, but also of other sources.

In addition to skepticism about historical sources, what other historical methods my students learn? Along the way they learn how to do archival research at the National Archives and the Library of Congress. They learn how to work with a variety of original sources, including naval records, census records, manuscript sources from the U.S. Cutter Service (now the Coast Guard), images, letters, diaries, maps, and historical newspapers. And they learned how to do something that von Ranke first insisted upon—the use of multiple sources in order to check the consistency of accounts in each source. After all, if their "true facts" did not triangulate properly, then their hoaxes would be more easily exposed for what they were. They had to portray Edwards Owens's or Joseph Scafe's world as it actually was, even if neither man existed in that world. And it turns out, they liked doing this sort of serious historical research.

As one of the students that worked on the historical background of Edward (making sure there weren't any anachronisms), it was a lot of genuine research—going through census records, looking up specifics in the regions we were placing Edward, and the like. I feel very knowledgeable in the ways of Coastal Virginia after the Civil War now. It's not like we were filling our minds with information that was completely bogus. We were studying real time periods, real situations and real conditions in order to make this work. This was probably the most exciting part for me.[46]

In addition to learning to work with this variety of sources and to use them for the purposes of triangulation, the students also learn that the creation of history is a collaborative endeavor. They work together in class, but they also learn the value of calling upon the expertise of others. Once the first group of students decided on their hoax they contacted one of our graduate students who is an expert in underwater archaeology, and another who wrote her master's thesis on law enforcement in Virginia during the nineteenth century. Being able to ask these historians questions moved the project along much more rapidly than would have been the case if the students tried to do all the work on their own—a valuable lesson indeed. Each group also learned many new skills in the production of historical knowledge in the digital world. In addition to Jane's blog (for which the members of that group all wrote drafts, but one student wrote in her own voice), they learned how to scan or download and then manipulate images, how to write and edit *Wikipedia* entries, basic video scripting and production, and how to find an audience, albeit a small one, by visiting various websites and posting notices about Jane's project. They also played extensively in the sandbox they were most comfortable in—Jane had a Facebook page and a YouTube channel. The students in the second iteration of the course learned all of these skills, as well as how to work, albeit unsuccessfully, with Reddit.

How many history courses take their discussion of ethics beyond a unit on plagiarism of the small and large variety? In such units, students are generally treated to admonitory lectures on student plagiarism (especially copying and pasting from websites), and on such bigger stories as the plagiarism controversies swirling around the work of such popular historians as Stephen F. Ambrose or Doris Kearns Goodwin.[47] The message of such units is clear—plagiarism is bad, bad, bad, and should be avoided at all costs. Who could disagree?[48] But such units do not really get to the heart of ethics in historical inquiry because they touch on only one, admittedly important, aspect of those ethics. My students have to grapple with much more difficult ethical issues—not the least of which is what it means to create a lie and purvey it on their own website, but also on the websites of others, such as *Wikipedia*. After all, is not one of the primary obligations of the historian to tell the truth about the past? Much of the work of historians is directed at "setting the record straight" in the face of fantasy versions of the past that correspond to the evidentiary record to some greater or lesser degree. Historians set themselves and their work against myth and imperfect memory in the hope that somehow histories we have written will convince our audiences of the truth of what we say in the face of outright lies, exaggerations, shadings, and other less accurate versions of what happened in the past.[49] If there is some sort of historians' Hippocratic oath compelling us to always tell the truth (or at least the truth as we know it), then my students and I violated that oath.

But the nature of "historical truth" is one that can certainly be debated—and is debated almost constantly by historians. For instance, is it "true" that daily life in medieval Europe was dominated by religious observance, or is this "truth" one we accept because the greatest store of evidence available to us about that daily life comes to us from a small circle of elite chroniclers who had a vested interest in playing up the importance of religion in daily life? Which account of the past is more "true"—the one that focuses on the accomplishments of leaders of a state, or the one that focuses on the accomplishments of the masses? Historians debate such "truths" constantly, and students, who want to know which account of the past is "best" or "most correct," struggle to understand how five historians can look at the same evidence and write five different books. Teaching them how to negotiate through this maze of competing truth claims is one of the goals of most methods and/or historiography courses, but many of the historians I have spoken with who try to teach introductions to historiography report that lessons about historiography are even more difficult to impart than lessons about types of evidence and how to work with them.

I decided to tackle the problem of helping students sort through competing truth claims by having my students create their own (false) version of historical truth. To do that, they had to imbed their work in existing histories that the students assumed to be as accurate as the authors of those works could make them. In this way they saw just how difficult it is to determine which truth claims should hold sway over others. Intentional fabrication is certainly very different from asserting that our version of the past was more correct or accurate than yours. Therefore, I challenged my students to think about whether or not we were crossing an ethical

Rubicon that we really should not be crossing. To have this conversation at all we had to discuss the whole business of historiography and competing truth claims, if only to decide how far removed our project was from the debates among historians. Engaging historiography from the space of intentional fabrication turned out to be surprisingly productive. Because my students knew they were on one end of a truth-falsehood continuum, they could then move along that continuum to decide where the dividing line between deliberate falsehood and something one of them called "just competing interpretations" could be found. To put it another way, they knew they were lying, and therefore had to figure out how to tell where deliberate lying about the past ended and legitimate argument about the past began—a useful distinction to be able to draw. We never found that exact point, but discussed examples such as the denial of the Holocaust as exemplars of the distinction we were trying to draw. Once we were satisfied that we understood something about that distinction, it was still up to the students to decide how far to go in their fabrication of the historical record.

Admittedly, I did not give them a choice about whether or not to create a hoax, but this aspect of the course is clearly stated in the syllabus and so students uncomfortable with the entire project could have dropped the class at the outset of the semester. To the best of my knowledge, no student dropped the class. This is not to say that students were completely comfortable with intentional fabrication of the historical record—some were, some were not. The important thing is that we talked about it a lot. And I am not a believer in the idea that education is supposed to be completely comfortable for students at all times, so the fact that my students were uncomfortable at various points in the semester was not a bad result from where I sat. In fact, ethical concerns were a part of our discussions in class almost every session once work on the hoax began. In the end, the distinction that made it possible for several students each semester to feel more comfortable with the hoax was thinking of it as humor or satire rather than "serious history." We never intended the hoax to last forever and knew we were going to expose our hoax as falsehood at the end of the semester, so it was not as though we were creating "zombie facts" and turning them loose forever. Knowing that the hoax would end made it easier to see the entire project as humor rather than a lie . . . more like what one might find in the *Onion*, rather than what one would find in a book trying to convince readers of a deliberately false version of the past.

Also, it seems to me that if we are going to turn our students loose to create historical content online—factual or fabricated—we have to have a serious conversation about ethics in the digital realm. For example, if they are going to be remixing the work of others and then claiming it, all or in part, as their own, where does remixing cross the line into plagiarism. At what point does "sampling" become "copying"? How much of someone else's work can be used without violating copyright restrictions the original author may have placed on the work? In a world where anything online seems to be available for free download (at least to many students), what are the nuances between a blanket Creative Commons license and an Attribution-NonCommercial-ShareAlike license? These questions and others like them can significantly complicate our discussions of plagiarism and are thus very important to have if we are going to ask our students to work in the digital space.

Once the class had debated the largest ethical issue—were we doing the right or wrong thing—then the students had to consider even thornier questions such as which subjects were out-of-bounds for their hoax, the specifics of copyright law, and responsible use of computing policies—subjects sure to elicit fluttering eyelids and perhaps even some drooling on the desk from the average student. I gave the students some specific limits about what they could not select for their hoax. For instance, one out-of-bounds topic my students readily agreed on was anything to do with medicine or health. Too many people rely on the Internet for information about health and health care, and so there would be nothing funny about creating a hoax in this domain. In the end, our list of other topics unavailable for hoaxing included anything that might have caused someone to send us money (wire fraud under U.S. law), anything to do with national security (I had no desire to visit Guantanamo, Cuba), and anything to do with the Civil War. Why the Civil War? That was a practical rather than ethical decision, because the community of historians, professional and amateur, devoted to the study of the Civil War is so large and their knowledge of the details of this conflict is so extensive and precise, we decided that there was no chance of perpetrating a successful Civil War hoax. Anything the students tried to do would be exposed almost instantly. Finally, I insisted that any hoax created would not violate the university's responsible use of computing policy, because I had no desire to be censured or fired as a result of a student project. This latter stipulation ruled out, for instance, any hoax that had to do with pornography or gambling. With the boundaries of the hoax firmly established, my students were then free to create any hoax they might think up.

That my students learned to think critically about such ethical issues is evident in what one student wrote in her personal blog.

> Ethically, the only doubt I have regarding my own participation in this project is the e-mail I sent to the writer of [the *USAToday* blog] Pop Candy. I do not exactly regret that action, but I do question it every time I think of it. Though I did not personally know this woman, I purposefully set out to deceive her for my own gains, taking advantage of the trust she has in her readers. I apologize for taking advantage of her trust in such a way.[50]

In the aftermath of the first hoax's exposure, another ethical issue arose that confirmed for me the importance of having cut off the hoax at the end of the semester so that we still had time to discuss the controversy that began to emerge as we dispersed for the 2008–9 winter break. Because ethical considerations were so much a part of what we discussed all semester, had we not had a little time to reflect on the response of those hoaxed once they found out they were victims, I think an important lesson of the semester would have been lost. The 2012 students were able to revisit this issue, especially in light of the brief media storm that followed the completion of the course.

Finally, my students all learned that creating history, whether it is "real" history or a hoax, is hard, and takes a lot of work. In the aftermath of the course, the student just quoted reflected on the project.

> I would like to say that all the details fell into place, but they didn't. We all worked and pushed them into place step by step. It was hard. Most definitely the hardest project I've ever worked on. We were entirely self-motivated in our groups. We had to figure out what needed to be doing before we could do it, and had to figure out entirely how to approach each step.[51]

But from my perspective, the most important lesson they learn is that history can be fun after all. This is a class in which the students showed up for class early and stayed late, remained engaged throughout the class sessions, worked in small groups outside of class, and laughed throughout the semester.

The additional issue that arose after the exposure of the first hoax is less a part of the main story of the class and the student learning results. But given that a number of historians, librarians, and others argued that the class design was inappropriate to a university setting, the question of whether or not the class is appropriate seems worth describing.[52] At issue was what one author termed "academic trust networks": the web of social networks (blogs, Twitter, discussion forums, etc.) that academics and others increasingly rely on to help us find and evaluate information.

> Online information increasingly exists in a context that provides us with a wealth of information about how that information is positioned within a larger conversation. When I find something of interest online, I do not only evaluate it's [sic] face-value worth; I evaluate it in terms of who else I know is linking to it, talking about it, critiquing it.[53]

Much of the criticism or support for the results of that first version of the course revolved around the issue of what my students' work had exposed about the reliance of academics (and others) on social networks as trusted sources of information. At one end of the continuum of this conversation was the argument that by encouraging my students to create a hoax and then purvey it in these trust networks, I had violated a basic tenet (or two) of my own professional community.[54] At the other end of the continuum was the argument that academics (especially academics) should know better than to accept what they find online at face value.[55] In chapter 2, I explained the importance of teaching students sophisticated searching skills—skills that transcend simple keyword searches in a search engine. That so many academics were taken in by the Edward Owens/Jane Browning hoax indicates just how far we have to go when it comes to teaching these skills to students. If we do not deploy them in our professional lives, how can our students be expected to take us seriously when we tell them that they must deploy such skills in their own academic work?

To my knowledge, none of the scholars and teachers who wrote about Jane and her pirate project employed tests such as a "WhoIs" lookup. If they had, they would have found that the domain did not belong to a student named Jane Browning, but to someone at George Mason University named Theodore Kelly, with the email tkelly7@gmu.edu and the telephone number 703-993-2152; in other words, me. A more careful reader of the WhoIs.com data would indicate that the domain was created on October 22, 2008. Given that Jane's first post in her blog was dated September 3, 2008, this more careful reader might have noticed something a little fishy. The question for those interested in the idea of academic trust networks is whether or not participants in those trust networks should be held to the same information literacy standards we expect from students? Because the point of the class was to teach my students some things worth knowing about historical methods, I think I will let one of them have the last word on this particular issue.

> I don't regret the trust networks we violated only because those that we violated didn't do their jobs as historians, they didn't do their research, they didn't check their facts, they took what we presented them at face value because they wanted to believe in the project that we had created. (Which in my opinion is why so many hoaxes work, just look at the Hitler diaries, reputations and careers were ruined because people wanted to believe.) Some of them claimed that they did not look at our hoax closely because they were looking at it not for its value as a history project, but instead because it was a techonology [*sic*] based history project . . .[56]

If the results of an unscientific, not very random survey I have done of colleagues at several institutions are correct and historical methods courses do need a new approach in this age of digital media, Lying About the Past offers one possible approach to the recasting of this course. Pedagogical strategies that disrupt our comfortable views of how a discipline should be taught can be unsettling. My approach to this rewrite of the methods course was certainly controversial and not to everyone's taste, as evidenced by the various public and private responses to the course cited earlier. Even my own department found the course to be more than they were comfortable with, ultimately deciding in November 2012 that I could no longer teach it. As mentioned earlier, I am not suggesting that a hoax course, or even a course that centers on being playful, is the only possible solution. But I did come away from the two iterations of the course with the belief that any recasting of the methods course needs to retain the elements of historical thinking we hold dear, but also needs to bring them to students in ways that are more in tune with the lives they live now and will live after graduation.

What can we expect from our students in the future? I think it is fair to say that right now in 2013, most history students lack clear guidance from their professors when it comes to creating history in digital media. Given this lack of guidance, I think we can anticipate two results. The first will be that the majority of our students will go on producing history the way we did and the way our professors before us did—they will write papers, some of which we are proud of, most of which we are satisfied with, and some of which frustrate us beyond belief. Sometimes our students will really enjoy writing those papers and will be as proud of the results as we are. Other times they will be bored senseless by yet another five- or ten-page paper, with a thesis, just the right number of sources, and a conclusion supported by evidence in the footnotes. By the time they obtain their history degrees, I think it is a safe bet that our students will have written at least as many papers that did not thrill them as papers that did. And what will they do with those papers after graduation? Will they show them to future employers—"Look what a great paper I can write!"—or will they file them away on a backup drive and forget about them? I suspect the latter will almost always be the case. But at least we can feel comforted in the knowledge that we have taught them how to do history the way it has been done for decades, even centuries, and von Ranke will smile down upon us.

The second result I think we can expect—and the one that is certainly emerging without any guidance from us—is that more and more of our students will begin to experiment with new forms of historical knowledge production—whether the mash-ups and remixes discussed earlier, or the more out-there work of Bill Turkel and his graduate students in their Lab For Humanistic Fabrication.[57] How would Turkel's ideas work in practice? Imagine that you are teaching a course on the pre-Columbian Americas that included a week devoted to the architectural feats of the various pre-Columbian civilizations. In the 1970s or 1980s you might have brought your slide projector to class and shown students images of structures such as the Mayan great pyramid at Chichen Itza in Mexico. At some point in the past decade or so that slide project was replaced by an Internet connection, and so you could show your students (or ask them to go find) various online images and videos of the pyramid. But even the best photographs and videos are not the same as being able to touch the pyramid itself. As much as you might like to, you cannot take your students to the Yucatán just to see this structure, but it is possible to ask them to print a replica and bring it to class.[58] Three-dimensional printing has been possible for several years now with such tools as the MakerBot, and with such a tool students can build sophisticated (but small) physical copies of any object from the past, so long as we have photographs of it from various perspectives. Plans and downloadable schematics for structures such as the pyramid at Chichen Itza, a gothic cathedral, or Stonehenge are all available online.[59]

Learning to use tools such as the MakerBot is not as simple as learning how to start a class blog, but it is worth remembering that ten or fifteen years ago, creating websites and online journals was not a simple process, and required a fair amount of training. It is reasonable to assume that a decade from now, three-dimensional printing will be as user friendly as website creation is today. The challenges and opportunities posed by such things as three-dimensional printing of objects from the past indicates the degree to which new vistas for teaching and learning are constantly opening before of us. Some of our students may already be able to do interesting and creative things with tools such as MakerBot—or others we have not seen. For now it is enough that we know such tools exist, but before long it will be up to us to guide them in ways they can use these tools to learn about the past—to make history on their own. None of us learned how to do this sort of work in graduate school, but that should not prevent us from learning how to teach students to make the most of the advantages technology offers them.

Conclusion

Because the digital realm is a space of rapid change, this book could never be more than a snapshot of that realm at a given moment. Between the time I began writing in 2009 and the winter of 2011 when I finished the full draft of the manuscript, much had already changed in the world of digital history. Some of those changes needed to be incorporated into the book, some did not, but all had to be considered. For instance, when I began writing the book, the mining of digital imagery was still in its infancy, but by the summer of 2011 a number of important developments in that field have accelerated the pace at which historians can expect to be able to do sophisticated mining of large databases of photographs and other images. I had to rewrite that entire section of the book twice along the way. When I finished the draft of this book no one had ever heard of a massive open online course (MOOC), but now it seems that MOOCs have taken over the conversation about teachers, learning, and technology. But even as the technology upon which we rely and what that technology can do for us changes rapidly, there are many things that will not change, or at least will not change much, in the teaching and learning of history in this digital age.

I think it is safe to say that history will remain an essential part of the school and university curriculum for as long as any of us will live. Too many people are interested in the past and too many others believe that a knowledge of history is essential to the smooth functioning of a modern democratic society for us to have to worry too much about a precipitous decline in the fortunes of our profession. But questions remain. Will history maintain its place in that curriculum, or continue to slip in terms of its overall popularity and the resources it commands in the face of competition from the STEM disciplines (science, technology, engineering, and mathematics)? As I have indicated a number of times throughout this book, I believe that unless we muster the will to reconceptualize the way we teach students about the past, taking into account the new realities of the digital world and the many and varied ways our students work, think, and live in that world, we are in trouble. I do not think that trouble would ever spell the end of history as a discipline, for the reasons just cited, but I do think we need to consider whether or not we are in danger of losing a substantial portion of our natural audience. And we do have a natural audience. Many students are just plain interested in history and so are willing to spend time in one or more of our classes even if they do not choose to major in history. Whether we teach them once or many times depends, at least in part, on the success we have in making our discipline relevant to the world they live in and plan to live in after graduation.

We can also count on the fact that the number of available digital historical sources will continue to increase at a rapid rate. As more and more of the national cultural and historical collections around the world are digitized, marked up, and made available to anyone who wants to use them, the incredible amount of historical content that will be available to us and to students will be such that even thinking our way around its edges will be an existential experience akin to standing on the beach and trying to make sense of the entirety of the world's oceans. The billions of historical sources out there for us to work with—more and more of which will be marked up with XML coding—will simply be too much to contemplate or reasonably consider working with. It used to be a commonplace to talk about trying to get a drink from the fire hose that is the Internet. Going forward from 2013 a better analogy might be trying to get a drink from one of the mammoth waves of Hawaii's Banzai Pipeline as it crashes down on your head. For this reason, where just a decade ago we had to teach students how to find enough primary sources to do interesting and original work, today we need to teach them how to pare down the results of their searches for such sources to something manageable in the context of a semester or a quarter.

There is no reason for us to believe that our students will suddenly stop being enthusiastic creators of online content. Survey after survey of the behavior of youth indicates that their love affair with creating online content is still waxing. What we cannot say with any certainty is how and where they will indulge their creative impulses. In 2013, Facebook and

YouTube are the two most common places where young people create content for others to see, use, and modify, but as anyone who studies youth culture will tell you, that culture is famously fickle. Who can say whether these two websites, one founded in 2004 and the other in 2005, will be as popular in seven years as they are today? It is instructive to remember that in 2006 MySpace dominated the world of social media and commanded a then-astronomical purchase price from Rupert Murdoch's NewsCorp. At the peak of its popularity, MySpace was growing by almost 300,000 users per day, but by 2011, MySpace was hemorrhaging 1 million users a month.[1] Before MySpace, there was Friendster, which discontinued its social networking accounts in May 2011, reconfiguring itself for a life in the gaming industry.[2] In late August 2012 President Obama held an "Ask Me Anything" session on Reddit that drew more than 2.5 million unique page views and more than 23,000 comments in one hour and in October 2012 Facebook announced that their site had surpassed the one billion member threshold. Among the things historians know is that all dominance is fleeting, and so it is a safe bet that a decade from now web platforms other than the ones that students rely on will be the places to be, to play, to work, and to create. But wherever they do it, it is also a safe bet that they will continue to create content at a rate that surprises us.

One reason it seems to be such a safe bet that young people will continue creating content online at ever greater rates is that the tools necessary for that creation keep getting easier to use and cheaper. In the preface I described having to learn to write my own HTML code to put my class syllabus online. When Netscape Composer hit the market in 1997, I was thrilled, because suddenly I could let the software help me create web pages without my needing to acquire more coding skills. The following spring, Dreamweaver appeared and made my life even easier (albeit a bit more expensive), because the software's interface not only helped me build web pages, it also helped me build entire websites in a much more organized manner. Ever since, the tools for making and maintaining online content have gotten easier and easier to use. Consider, for a moment, how difficult it was to geolocate historical content and display it through a web browser. Although the desktop version of the ArcGIS software had been available since 1999, this software was designed for those with a background in geographic information systems rather than the casual user (including historians and their students) who wanted to mash up historical and geographic datasets. Google changed the terms of this particular game when they made their Maps API available to the general public in 2005.[3] The Google Maps API has proven to be the most popular API embedded on websites worldwide, is now available on most mobile devices and, as mentioned earlier, is being used by hundreds, if not thousands, of historians, students of history, and casual enthusiasts for the past to create various mash-ups of historical and geographic data. In 2011 the Open Knowledge Project released a simple tool for creating even more sophisticated mash-ups of historical and geographic data—Weaving History—that links the Google Maps API with the popular open-source time line creator, Simile, created at MIT.[4] Now, with just a few clicks of a mouse and a few minutes of typing, anyone can create the kind of reasonably sophisticated historical map that only professionals could make a few years ago.

The world we are preparing our students to enter continues to change almost as rapidly. Employment opportunities with some sort of obvious and direct connection to a degree in history used to fall into a relatively small number of categories, including education, museums and archives, or work at historic sites. Over the decades many history students have seen their major as strong preparation for a career in education, law, politics, or government service. All of these options continue to be there for history students, and there is nothing to indicate that this will change much in the coming decade. However, the digital revolution has opened up many new, exciting, and often lucrative opportunities for students that history departments only rarely take into account. For example, organizations ranging from large corporations, to cultural institutions, to government agencies are all but desperate to hire digital archivists—at starting salaries in the same range as those paid to beginning assistant professors of history. Working with and in archives is something history departments typically spend a fair amount of time teaching our students how to do, but only a few departments around the country offer students an opportunity to develop the kinds of sophisticated digital archiving skills that are required to claim one of these jobs.

Finally, I think we can safely assume that if we find ways to turn students loose—to give them room to create history the ways they want rather than the ways we insist on—while still maintaining our standards and remaining true to our learning goals, our students will surprise us more and more often with what they produce. It may be a video like the Tank Man mash-up discussed earlier; it may be a new use for a mobile app; it might be a series of blog posts; it might be a map overlay; or it might be a combination of any or all of these. While it is impossible to say what exactly they might produce if we give their creative impulses more room to maneuver, I think it is also a safe bet that if we do not give them this sort of creative license, only rarely will they surprise us with what they do. Certainly, we will continue to receive carefully crafted, well-researched, and well-argued essays from our best students. What we will not see is the kind of creative work—work that takes partial or full advantage of the potential of the digital realm—that they are actually capable of. Students study history because they want to, not because it is a path to fortune or fame. The time has come for us to recognize that our students have a lot to teach us about the past and how we can combine what we know with what they know to make history together.

Notes

Preface

1. T. Mills Kelly, "For Better or Worse? The Marriage of the Web and Classroom," *Journal of the Association for History and Computing* 3, no. 2 (August 2000), http://mcel.pacificu.edu/jahc/2000/issue2/articles/kelly/.

2. For more on this topic, see Cathy Davidson, "Mobile Humanities," *HASTAC*, May 26, 2008; "Mobile Social History/Memory Digital History Project," John Nicholas Brown Center, http://proteus.brown.edu/jnbc/817; Cameron Blevins, "The Mobile Historian," *historying*. http://historying.org/2009/05/03/the-mobile-historian/.

Acknowledgments

1. The best introduction to Roy's life and work is Roy Rosenzweig, *Clio Wired: The Future of the Past in the Digital Age* (New York: Columbia University Press, 2011).

Introduction

1. "21 Nazi Chiefs Guilty," *Nuremberg Trials* 1946/10/8, 2006, http://www.youtube.com/watch?v=xcudlm6tPao&feature=youtube_gdata. Accessed July 27, 2010.

2. See, for example, T. Mills Kelly, "Tomorrow's Yesterdays: Teaching History in the Digital Age," in *Brave New Classrooms: Educational Democracy and the Internet*, ed. Mark Pegrum and Joe Lockard (New York: Peter Lang, 2006), 213–24; "Remaking Liberal Education. The Challenges of New Media," *Academe* (January–February 2003): 28–31; and "For Better or Worse?"

3. Fred Morrow Fling and Howard Walter Caldwell, *Studies in European and American History* (J. H. Miller, 1897), 9–10.

4. Simon Spradlin, *Studies in the History of History Teaching* (Norman: University of Oklahoma Press, 1936), 81.

5. Nicholas Kulish, "Author, 17, Says It's 'Mixing,' Not Plagiarism," *New York Times,* February 12, 2010, http://www.nytimes.com/2010/02/12/world/europe/12germany.html.

6. See, for instance, Edward H. Carr, "The Historian and His Facts," in *What is History?* (New York: Alfred A. Knopf, 1962), 3–35, and Carl Becker, "Everyman His Own Historian," *American Historical Review* 37, no. 2 (December 1931): 221–36.

7. Errol Morris, "Which Came First, the Chicken or the Egg? (Part One)," *Opinionator,* September 25, 2007, http://opinionator.blogs.nytimes.com/2007/09/25/which-came-first-the-chicken-or-the-egg-part-one/; "Does the Camera Ever Lie?" *American Memory Project,* Library of Congress, http://memory.loc.gov/ammem/cwphtml/cwpcam/cwcam1.html. Accessed June 4, 2011.

8. Thomas S. Kuhn, *The Structure of Scientific Revolutions,* 3rd ed. (Chicago: University of Chicago Press, 1996), 92.

9. Robert Townsend, "Assimilation of New Media into History Teaching: Some Snapshots from the Edge," *Perspectives* 48, no. 9 (December 2010): 24–26.

10. http://digitalhistory.wikispot.org/Interactive_Ambient_and_Tangible_Devices_for_Knowledge_Mobilization. Accessed February 25, 2010.

11. "More Than Just Digital Quilting," *Economist*, December 3, 2011, 3–4.

12. The image of the stencil is at http://www.flickr.com/photos/tmkelly/4053321333/. More information on the Craft ROBO is available at http://www.graphteccorp.com/craftrobo/.

13. Doug Rohrer and Harold Pashler, "Recent Research on Human Learning Challenges Conventional Instructional Strategies," *Educational Researcher* 39 (2010): 406–12.

14. *Digital Humanities Now,* http://digitalhumanitiesnow.org/.

15. In addition to the sources cited earlier, see Max Farrand, "Report of the Conference on History in the College Curriculum," American Historical Association (1906), and Charles Homer Haskins "Report of the Conference on the First Year of College Work in History," American Historical Association (1906). For a useful review of the relationship between academic historians and the teaching of history in the schools, see Robert Orrill and Linn Shapiro, "From Bold Beginnings to an Uncertain Future: The Discipline of History and History Education," *American Historical Review,* 110, no. 3 (2005), and Robert Townsend, "Making History: Scholarship and Professionalization in the Discipline, 1880–1940" (PhD diss., George Mason University, 2009).

16. Lion F. Gardiner, "Why We Must Change: The Research Evidence," *Thought & Action* 14, no. 1 (Spring 1998): 78. See also L. Dee Fink, *Creating Significant Learning Experiences* (San Francisco: Jossey-Bass, 2003), 4–10.

17. Gardiner, "Why We Must Change," 4–10.

18. Lendol Calder, "Uncoverage: Toward a Signature Pedagogy for the History

Survey," *Journal of American History* 92, no. 4 (March 2006), http://www.historyco
operative.org/journals/jah/92.4/calder.html.

19. Dennis Jacobs, "An Alternative Approach to General Chemistry," http://
gallery.carnegiefoundation.org/collections/castl_he/djacobs/index2.htm. Accessed
December 1, 2011.

20. Daniel J. Cohen, "By the Book: Assessing the Place of Textbooks in U.S.
Survey Courses," *Journal of American History* 91, no. 4 (March 2005), http://www
.historycooperative.org/journals/jah/91.4/cohen.html.

21. Townsend, "Assimilation of New Media," 26.

22. Sarah Horton, *Web Teaching Guide* (New Haven, CT: Yale University Press,
2000), xi.

23. Paul Taylor and Scott Keeter, *Millennials: Confident. Connected. Open to
Change.—Pew Social & Demographic Trends* (Pew Research Center, February 2010),
25–29, http://pewsocialtrends.org/pubs/751/millennials-confident-connected-open-
to-change.

24. Fred Stutzman, *Student Life on the Facebook* (Chapel Hill, NC, January 8,
2006), http://fredstutzman.com/pubs/stutzman_wp3.pdf.

25. Mizuko Ito et al., *Hanging Out, Messing Around, and Geeking Out* (Cambridge, MA: MIT Press, 2009), 244.

Chapter 1

1. Robert Orrill and Linn Shapiro, "From Bold Beginnings to an Uncertain Future: The Discipline of History and History Education," *American Historical Review*
110, no. 3 (June 2005), http://www.historycooperative.org/journals/ahr/110.3/orrill
.html.

2. Burke Aaron Hinsdale, *How to Study and Teach History* (New York: D. Appleton and Company, 1897), 63–64.

3. Hinsdale, *How to Study and Teach History,* 61.

4. Charles H. Haskins, "Report of the Conference on the First Year of College
Work in History," American Historical Association (1906), 147.

5. J. Carleton Bell, "Editorials: The Historic Sense," *Journal of Educational Psychology* 8, no. 5 (May 1917): 318. See also Sam Wineburg, "Crazy for History," *Journal
of American History* (March 2004), jah/90.4/wineburg.html. Accessed February 12,
2010.

6. Bell, "The Historic Sense," 318.

7. For more on the history of the historical profession, see Robert Townsend,
Making History: Scholarship and Professionalization in the Discipline, 1880–1940, publication forthcoming, fall 2012 (University of Chicago Press).

8. See, for example, "Making History and Civics a Priority," *Washington Post,*
June 17, 2011, http://www.washingtonpost.com/opinions/making-history-a-civics-
a-priority/2011/06/17/AGb1tYZH_story.html.

9. "Slade Gorton Speech on the Proposed National History Standards," *C-SPAN*, January 18, 1995, http://www.c-spanarchives.org/congress/?q=node/7753 1&id=7079046.

10. Stéphane Lévesque, *Thinking Historically: Educating Students for the Twenty-First Century* (Toronto: University of Toronto Press, 2008), 6; Pierre Nora and Lawrence D. Kritzman, *Realms of Memory: Conflicts and Divisions* (New York: Columbia University Press, 1996), 3.

11. Mills Kelly, "Welcome to Minsk, Florida," *Edwired,* September 6, 2006, http://edwired.org/?p=91.

12. See, for example, Gary B Nash, *History on Trial: Culture Wars and the Teaching of the Past,* 1st ed. (New York: Alfred A. Knopf, 1997).

13. Michael Birnbaum, "A Message for Washington on Schools: Don't Mess with Texas," *Washington Post,* March 31, 2010, http://www.washingtonpost.com/wp-dyn/content/article/2010/03/31/AR2010033103989.html. The comments in the online version of this story help to highlight the polarized nature of such debates in American society: http://www.washingtonpost.com/wp-dyn/content/article/2010/03/31/AR2010033103989_Comments.html.

14. Peter Seixas, "Schweigen! die Kinder!," in *Knowing, Teaching and Learning History: National and International Perspectives* (New York: New York University Press, 2000), 23.

15. Sam Wineburg, "Crazy for History," *Journal of American History* 90, no. 4 (March 2004): 1401–14.

16. Robert B. Bain, "Into the Breach: Using Research and Theory to Shape History Instruction," in *Knowing, Teaching and Learning History: National and International Perspectives* (New York: New York University Press, 2000), 337; David Pace, "The Amateur in the Operating Room: History and the Scholarship of Teaching and Learning," *American Historical Review* 109, no. 4 (October 2004), http://www.historycooperative.org/journals/ahr/109.4/pace.html.

17. "Women at Odds over Suffrage Question," *New York Times,* March 17, 1907.

18. David Lowenthal, "Dilemmas and Delights of Learning History," in *Knowing, Teaching and Learning History: National and International Perspectives* (New York: New York University Press, 2000), 74.

19. James Axtell, "The Pleasures of Teaching History," *History Teacher* 34, no. 4 (August 2001), http://www.historycooperative.org/journals/ht/34.4/axtell.html.

20. Bertold Brecht, *Brecht on Theatre: The Development of an Aesthetic,* 13th ed. (New York: Hill & Wang, 1977), 192.

21. Samuel S. Wineburg, *Historical Thinking and Other Unnatural Acts: Charting the Future of Teaching the Past* (Philadelphia: Temple University Press, 2001), 242–48.

22. Axtell, "The Pleasures of Teaching History."

23. Wineburg, *Historical Thinking and Other Unnatural Acts,* 5.

24. Sam Wineburg et al., "Forrest Gump and the Future of Teaching the Past," *Phi Delta Kappan* 89, no. 3 (November 2007): 233–55; Pace, "The Amateur in the Operating Room."

25. Carl Wieman and Kathleen Perkins, "Transforming Physics Education," *Physics Today* 58, no. 11 (2005): 36–41.

26. "Historical Thinking Matters," http://historicalthinkingmatters.org/.

27. Daisy Martin and Sam Wineburg, "Seeing Thinking on the Web," *History Teacher* 41, no. 3 (May 2008), http://www.historycooperative.org.mutex.gmu.edu/journals/ht/41.3/martin.html.

28. Wieman and Perkins, "Transforming Physics Education," 3.

29. Bain, "Into the Breach: Using Research and Theory to Shape History Instruction," 331; Lévesque, *Thinking Historically*, 27.

30. Edward H. Carr, *What Is History?* (New York: Alfred A. Knopf, 1962), 10–11.

31. Bain, "Into the Breach: Using Research and Theory to Shape History Instruction," 332.

32. Paul Ward, *Elements of Historical Thinking* (Washington, D.C: American Historical Association, 1971), 4–5.

33. Peter Novick, *That Noble Dream: The "Objectivity Question" and the American Historical Profession* (Cambridge: Cambridge University Press, 1988), 26–30; George G. Iggers and James M. Powell, eds., *Leopold Von Ranke and the Shaping of the Historical Discipline,* 1st ed. (Syracuse, NY: Syracuse University Press, 1990), xix–xx.

34. Lévesque, *Thinking Historically*, 27; Seixas, "Schweigen! die Kinder!," 24–25.

35. Wineburg, *Historical Thinking and Other Unnatural Acts,* 5.

36. *Jacobellis v. Ohio,* 378 U.S. 184, 197 (1964).

37. On the disconnect between our expectations and our students' expectations, see Gerald Graff, *Clueless in Academe: How Schooling Obscures the Life of the Mind* (New Haven, CT: Yale University Press, 2003).

38. James J. Weingartner, "Trophies of War: U.S. Troops and the Mutilation of Japanese War Dead, 1941–1945," *Pacific Historical Review* 61, no. 1 (February 1992): 53–67.

Chapter 2

1. John McClymer, *The AHA Guide to Teaching and Learning With New Media* (Washington, D.C: American Historical Association, 2005), 4–5.

2. *Information R/evolution,* 2007, http://www.youtube.com/watch?v=-4CV05HyAbM&feature=youtube_gdata.

3. Roy Rosenzweig, "Scarcity or Abundance? Preserving the Past in a Digital Era," *American Historical Review* 108, no. 3 (June 2003): 738.

4. "How Tweet It Is!: Library Acquires Entire Twitter Archive," *Library of Congress Blog,* http://blogs.loc.gov/loc/2010/04/how-tweet-it-is-library-acquires-entire-twitter-archive/.

5. http://marxists.org. Accessed May 11, 2010.

6. http://library.duke.edu/digitalcollections/adaccess/. Accessed May 11, 2010.

7. David Rumsey Map Collection, http://www.davidrumsey.com/ and http://www.lib.utexas.edu/maps/map_collection_guide.html. Accessed October 1, 2010.

8. George P. Landow, *Hypertext 2.0* (Baltimore: Johns Hopkins University Press, 1997), 183.

9. Alison J. Head, "Beyond Google: How Do Students Conduct Academic Research?," *First Monday* 12, no. 8 (August 2007), http://firstmonday.org/htbin/cgiwrap/bin/ojs/index.php/fm/article/view/1998; and Karl V. Fast and D. Grant Campbell, "'I Still Like Google': University Student Perceptions of Searching OPACs and the Web," in *Proceedings of the American Society for Information Science and Technology,* vol. 41, 2004, 138–46.

10. Rosenzweig, "Scarcity or Abundance?," 756.

11. José I. Castillo-Manzano and Lourdes López-Valpuestaa, "The Decline of the Traditional Travel Agent Model," *Transportation Research Part E: Logistics and Transportation Review* 46, no. 5 (September 2010): 639–49.

12. See comments on the post: *The Last American Pirate,* "Videos," http://lastamericanpirate.net/2008/12/03/videos/index.html. Accessed November 1, 2010.

13. *Edwired,* "Why I Won't Get Hired at Middlebury," http://edwired.org/2007/01/26/why-i-wont-get-hired-at-middlebury/. Accessed September 27, 2010.

14. Olga Rieger, "Search Engine Use Behavior of Students and Faculty: User Perceptions and Implications for Future Research," *First Monday* 14, no. 12 (December 2009), http://firstmonday.org/htbin/cgiwrap/bin/ojs/index.php/fm/article/view/2716/2385.

15. Flickr Commons: http://www.flickr.com/commons.

16. "Many Hands Make Light Work," *Flickr blog,* http://blog.flickr.net/en/2008/01/16/many-hands-make-light-work/.

17. On the Dublin Core Metadata Initiative, see http://dublincore.org/.

18. Michael J. Galgano, J. Chris Arndt, and Raymond M. Hyser, *Doing History: Research and Writing in the Digital Age,* 1st ed. (Boston: Wadsworth Publishing, 2007).

19. Stephen Ramsay, "The Hermeneutics of Screwing Around; or What You Do with a Million Books," unpublished paper, April 17, 2010.

20. *Red-Color News Soldier:* http://www.red-colornewssoldier.com/index.html. *Titoville:* http://www.titoville.com/. For reviews of these websites, see http://chnm.gmu.edu/worldhistorysources/d/348/whm.html and http://chnm.gmu.edu/worldhistorysources/d/43/whm.html. All accessed January 3, 2011.

21. *Tweeting the Civil War,* Washingtonpost.com: http://twitter.com/CivilWarwp/tweeting-the-civil-war. Accessed January 5, 2011.

22. *Tweeting the Civil War,* Washingtonpost.com: http://twitter.com/CivilWarwp/tweeting-the-civil-war. Accessed January 5, 2011.

23. Errol Morris, "Which Came First, the Chicken or the Egg? (Part One)," *Opinionator,* September 25, 2007, http://opinionator.blogs.nytimes.com/2007/09/25/which-came-first-the-chicken-or-the-egg-part-one/. Errol Morris, "Which Came First, the Chicken or the Egg? (Part Two)," *Opinionator,* October 23, 2007, http://opinionator.blogs.nytimes.com/2007/10/04/which-came-first-part-two/.

Errol Morris, "Which Came First, the Chicken or the Egg? (Part Three): Can George, Lionel and Marmaduke Help Us Order the Fenton Photographs?," *Opinionator*, http://opinionator.blogs.nytimes.com/2007/10/23/which-came-first-part-three-can-george-lionel-and-marmaduke-help-us-order-the-fenton-photographs/.

24. In our defense, we wrote this book at the behest of a publisher who wanted us to provide capsule reviews of websites already reviewed in our website, World History Sources (http://chnm.gmu.edu/worldhistorysources/), that could then be packaged with a textbook.

25. Wikiquote.org, "Adolf Hitler", http://en.wikiquote.org/wiki/Adolf_Hitler. Accessed May 3, 2010.

26. On the problems posed by websites such as this one for students, see Kristin Lehner, Kelly Schrum, and T. Mills Kelly, *World History Matters: A Student Guide to World History Online,* 1st ed. (New York: Bedford/St. Martin's, 2008).

27. Adolf Hitler Historical Museum, http://www.hitler.org. Accessed May 3, 2010.

28. See, for example, the library website resource page for Mount Mercy College (Cedar Rapids, IA): http://www.mtmercy.edu/busselibrary/desktop/holoc/holoc2.html, accessed May 3, 2010; the popular Fordham University Library Modern History Sourcebook: http://www.fordham.edu/halsall/mod/modsbook43.html.

29. http://www.randomhouse.com/catalog/display.pperl?isbn=9780385751063&view=rg. Accessed May 3, 2010.

30. "History Links," Professor Michael J. Morgan, Rose State College, Oklahoma: http://www.rose.edu/faculty/mmorgan/ww2Pres.htm. Accessed May 3, 2010.

31. "Adolf Hitler", *Newsweekopedia,* http://topics.newsweek.com/politics/adolf-hitler.htm. I say "unwittingly" here, because the link to the Museum website shows up on the *Newsweek* page in a list of "Web Search Results Powered by LiveSearch"—content ported into the site from elsewhere rather than placed on the site intentionally. Nevertheless, the uncritical way in which *Newsweek* reproduces links to such a website speaks volumes to the hazards of automated search and retrieval.

32. The issue of this particular website showing up so high in the Google search rankings was first aired by Randall Bytwerk on the H-German email discussion list on April 7, 2006. http://h-net.msu.edu/h-german. Bytwerk also published a similar piece on the History News Network (HNN) website on April 17, 2006, titled "Do Historians Have a Responsibility to Warn the Public About Misleading Websites?" http://hnn.us/articles/23723.html. Accessed May 3, 2010.

33. "About," *Making the History of 1989,* http://chnm.gmu.edu/1989/about. Accessed May 3, 2010.

34. http://www.archive.org/index.php.

35. http://web.archive.org/web/*/http://hitler.org.

36. http://web.archive.org/web/20010420090126/http://www.hitler.org/.

37. Roy Rosenzweig, "Digital Archives Are a Gift of Wisdom to Be Used Wisely," *Chronicle of Higher Education,* June 24, 2005.

38. http://digitool1.lva.lib.va.us, call number G3841.P15 1849 .M58. Accessed May 19, 2010.

39. Martin Luther King Jr. community page, Facebook.com. Accessed May 10, 2010, at 2:00 p.m. EST. I cite the date and time because these posts harvested from the Facebook community scroll constantly, and so disappear quickly from the main page.

40. Button offered for sale at http://www.toppun.com/Martin-Luther-King/Buttons/Everything-that-is-done-in-the-world-is-done-by-hope-Martin-Luther-King-Jr-BUTTON.html. Accessed May 11, 2010.

41. See http://www.youtube.com/watch?v=PbUtL_ovAJk, http://www.you tube.com/watch?v=o0FiCxZKuv8, and http://www.youtube.com/watch?v=cmO BbxgxKvo. A second version of the "I Have a Dream" speech showed up in third position. All accessed May 10, 2010.

42. For a useful comparison of the basic elements of these packages, see "Comparison of reference management software," *Wikipedia,* http://en.wikipedia.org/wiki/Comparison_of_reference_management_software, accessed December 27, 2011. Websites for these software packages are http://zotero.org, http://mendeley .com, and http://www.connotea.org/.

43. "Personalized Search for Everyone," *Official Google blog,* http://googleblog .blogspot.com/2009/12/personalized-search-for-everyone.html. Accessed December 27, 2011.

44. For more on this issue, see Eli Pariser, *The Filter Bubble. What the Internet Is Hiding from You* (New York: Viking, 2011).

Chapter 3

1. On the emergence of digital libraries, see Gregory Crane, "What Do You Do with a Million Books?," *D-Lib Magazine* 12, no. 3 (March 2006), http://digitalhu manities.org/dhq/vol/3/2/000041/000041.html.

2. At the founding of the new republic in 1918, Klofáč became the new state's first minister of defense while Kramář became the first foreign minister.

3. William J. Turkel, "Text Mining the DCB, Part 1," *Digital History Hacks (2005–8),* January 28, 2006, http://digitalhistoryhacks.blogspot.com/2006/01/text-mining-dcb-part-1.html.

4. "What Do You Do with a Million Books?"

5. Sam Wineburg, "Probing the Depths of Students' Historical Knowledge—Perspectives (March 1992)—American Historical Association," *Perspectives* 30 (March 1992), http://www.historians.org/perspectives/issues/1992/9203/9203TEC1.cfm.

6. "Be the Historian," *World History Sources,* http://chnm.gmu.edu/worldhis torysources/unpacking/acctsq2.php?account=no. Accessed December 3, 2010. For a second example of this Web 1.0 approach, see "Try it Yourself," *History Matters,* http://historymatters.gmu.edu/mse/letters/try5.html. Accessed December 3, 2010.

7. John Unsworth, "New Methods for Humanities Research" (lecture, the

Lyman Award Lecture, National Humanities Center, November 11, 2005), http://www3.isrl.illinois.edu/~unsworth/lyman.htm.

8. On recombinant documents, see William Gibson, "God's Little Toys," *Wired,* July 2005, http://www.wired.com/wired/archive/13.07/gibson.html; Daniel J. Cohen, "History and the Second Decade of the Web," *Rethinking History* 8, no. 2 (June 2004): 293–301.

9. Kevin Kelly, "Scan This Book!," *New York Times,* May 14, 2006, http://www.nytimes.com/2006/05/14/magazine/14publishing.html?pagewanted=4.

10. http://www.jstor.org/page/info/about/archives/facts.jsp. Accessed May 20, 2010.

11. http://www.lexisnexis.com/about-us. Accessed May 20, 2010.

12. http://www.europeana.eu/portal/aboutus.html. Accessed May 20, 2010.

13. http://www.proquest.com/en-US/catalogs/databases/detail/pq-hist-news.shtml. Accessed May 20, 2010.

14. Jeffrey Heer, Michael Bostock, and Vadim Ogievetsky, "A Tour through the Visualization Zoo—ACM Queue," *ACMQueue,* May 13, 2010, http://queue.acm.org/detail.cfm?id=1805128.

15. Mark Bauerlein, *The Dumbest Generation: How the Digital Age Stupefies Young Americans and Jeopardizes Our Future.* (New York: Penguin, 2009), 26. Barbara Tischler, "Teaching World History: Issues and Possibilities," *Perspectives* (October 2009), http://www.historians.org/perspectives/issues/2009/0910/0910tea4.cfm.

16. Dennis Reinhartz and Stephen E. Maizlish, *Essays on Walter Prescott Webb and the Teaching of History,* 1st ed. (College Station: Texas A&M University Press, 1985), 79–98.

17. For examples of how a geographer and a historian explain maps to students, see Joni Seager, "Maps," *World History Sources,* http://chnm.gmu.edu/worldhistorysources/unpacking/mapsmain.html, and Gerald Danzer, "Maps," *World History Sources,* http://chnm.gmu.edu/worldhistorysources/analyzing/maps/analyzingmapsintro.html. Both accessed May 27, 2010.

18. http://bbs.keyhole.com/ubb/ubbthreads.php?ubb=showflat&Number=1185352#Post1185352. Accessed June 3, 2010.

19. *Light and Shadows: Emma Goldman 1910–1916,* http://gray.ischool.berkeley.edu/emma/. Accessed May 15, 2010.

20. *NS-Crimes in Vienna,* http://www.ns-verbrechen.at/. Accessed January 7, 2011. This website no longer exists but can be viewed at the Internet Archive (archive.org).

21. *Digital Harlem: Everyday Life 1915–1930,* http://acl.arts.usyd.edu.au/harlem/. Accessed January 11, 2011.

22. "Hypercities," http://hypercities.com/. Accessed June 7, 2010.

23. Tim O'Reilly, "What Is Web 2.0—O'Reilly Media," *O'Reilly,* http://oreilly.com/web2/archive/what-is-web-20.html; Tim O'Reilly and John Battelle, "Web Squared: Web 2.0 Five Years On" (lecture, presented at the Web 2.0 Summit, San

Francisco, October 2009), http://www.web2summit.com/web2009/public/sched ule/detail/10194.

24. *Katrina pics in Flickr*, http://pipes.yahoo.com/pipes/pipe.info?_id=KjeIBsj N3BGfn99dl7okhQ.

25. *HistoryPin*, http://www.historypin.com/. As of June 27, 2011, almost 50,000 images had already been geotagged in this database, and some were organized into collections, such a one focusing on British royal weddings of the past.

26. See, for instance, David H. Pinkney, *The French Revolution of 1830* (Princeton, NJ: Princeton University Press, 1972), vii.

27. William Turkel, "Clustering with Compression," *Digital History Hacks (2005–8)*, June 27, 2007, http://digitalhistoryhacks.blogspot.com/2007/06/cluster ing-with-compression.html. Accessed June 7, 2010.

28. William Turkel, "Text Mining the DCB, Part 1," *Digital History Hacks (2005–8)*, January 28, 2006, http://digitalhistoryhacks.blogspot.com/2006/01/text-min ing-dcb-part-1.html.

29. Heer, Bostock, and Ogievetsky, "A Tour through the Visualization Zoo—ACM Queue."

30. That Hitler's rhetoric shifted according to his audience is an argument historians of the Nazi movement have made for decades. What is lacking, however, is a comprehensive analysis of all of Hitler's speeches from his appearance on the public stage to the outbreak of the war in 1939. Important studies, like William Sheridan Allen's *The Nazi Seizure of Power: The Experience of a Single German Town, 1922–1945*, (New York: F. Watts, 1984), make this argument, but are necessarily limited to small geographic areas because Allen did not have the advantage of being able to work with such a massive corpus of text.

31. Patricia Cohen, "Humanities Scholars Embrace Digital Technology," *New York Times*, November 16, 2010, http://www.nytimes.com/2010/11/17/ arts/17digital.html?_r=1; Dan Cohen, "Enhancing Historical Research with Text-Mining and Analysis Tools," dancohen.org, February 4, 2008, http://www.danco hen.org/2008/02/04/enhancing-historical-research-with-text-mining-and-analysis-tools/; Richard J. Cox, "Machines in the Archive: Technology and the Coming Transformation of Archival Reference," *First Monday* 12, no. 11 (November 2007), http://firstmonday.org/htbin/cgiwrap/bin/ojs/index.php/fm/article/view/2029.

32. http://manyeyes.alphaworks.ibm.com/manyeyes/.

33. Dan Cohen, "It's About Russia," dancohen.org, http://www.dancohen .org/2007/03/06/its-about-russia/. Accessed June 7, 2010.

34. "Visualizing Millions of Words," *Edwired.org*, December 17, 2010. Accessed December 8, 2011.

35. Dan Cohen, "10 Most Popular History Syllabi," dancohen.org, January 11, 2006, http://www.dancohen.org/blog/posts/10_most_popular_history_syllabi. Accessed June 10, 2010.

36. For more on the Syllabus Finder, see Daniel J. Cohen, "By the Book: Assessing the Place of Textbooks in U.S. Survey Courses," *Journal of American History*

91, no. 4 (March 2005), http://www.historycooperative.org/journals/jah/91.4/cohen .html.

37. Cited in Bei Yu, Stefan Kaufmann, and Daniel Diermeier, "Classifying Party Political Affiliation from Political Speech," *Journal of Information Technology & Politics* 5, no. 1 (2008): 33–49.

38. Yu, Kaufmann, and Diermeier, "Classifying Party Political Affiliation from Political Speech," 44–45.

39. Jeremy Douglass, "Software Studies: Cultural Pattern Recognition, or Seeing Through Images: Automatic Analysis of Visual Media and User Interactions," Softwarestudies.com, November 7, 2008, http://lab.softwarestudies.com/2008/05/ seeing-through-images-content-analysis.html.

40. Ching-chih Chen et al., "Digital Imagery for Significant Cultural and Historical Materials," *International Journal on Digital Libraries* 5 (2005): 279.

41. See, for instance, Thomas Deselaers and Vittorio Ferrari, "Global and Efficient Self-Similarity for Object Classification and Detection" (lecture, the IEEE Computer Vision and Pattern Recognition, San Francisco, 2010).

42. *PhotoDNA*, http://www.microsoft.com/presspass/presskits/photodna/. Accessed June 27, 2011.

43. "Dorothea Lange's 'Migrant Mother' Photographs in the Farm Security Administration Collection: An Overview—Guides, Reference Aids, and Finding Aids (Prints and Photographs Reading Room, Library of Congress)," http://www.loc .gov/rr/print/list/128_migm.html.

Chapter 4

1. For a quick summary of the history of printing, see Elizabeth L. Eisenstein, *The Printing Press as an Agent of Change: Communications and Cultural Transformations in Early-Modern Europe* (Cambridge: Cambridge University Press, 1979).

2. See, for instance, the PressForward initiative at the Center for History and New Media: http://pressforward.org/.

3. On the growing disconnect between historians and the general public, see Bob Thompson, "Lessons We May Be Doomed To Repeat; American Historians Talk About War, but Is Anyone Listening?" *Washington Post,* January 11, 2004; and "The Shrinking Historian," *Edwired,* October 10, 2007, http://edwired.org/2007/10/10/ the-shrinking-historian/. Accessed November 6, 2010.

4. "The Five Page Paper and the History Degree," *Edwired.org,* May 23, 2011.

5. Eisenstein, *The Printing Press as an Agent of Change.*

6. "85% of College Students Use Facebook," *TechCrunch,* September 7, 2005; on Facebook and college students, see fredstutzman.com.

7. Paul Taylor and Scott Keeter, *Millennials: Confident. Connected. Open to Change.—Pew Social & Demographic Trends* (Pew Research Center, February 2010), http://pewsocialtrends.org/pubs/751/millennials-confident-connected-open-to-change; and Mizuko Ito, Becky Herr-Stephenson, Dan Perkel, and Christo Sims,

eds., *Hanging Out, Messing Around, and Geeking Out: Kids Living and Learning with New Media* (Cambridge, MA: MIT Press, 2009).

8. On the impact of technologies on students and their writing, see J. David Bolter, *Remediation: Understanding New Media* (Cambridge, MA: MIT Press, 1999); J. David Bolter, *Writing Space: Computers, Hypertext, and the Remediation of Print,* 2nd ed. (Mahwah, NJ: Lawrence Erlbaum Associates, 2001).

9. Hart Research Associates, *Raising The Bar: Employers' Views On College Learning In The Wake Of The Economic Downturn* (Washington, D.C., January 2010).

10. "The Five Page Paper and the History Degree," *Edwired,* May 23, 2011, http://edwired.org/2011/05/23/the-five-page-paper-and-the-future-of-the-history-degree/. Accessed June 2, 2011.

11. For an example of a book originally written in chunks, see McKenzie Wark, *GAM3R 7H30RY* (Cambridge, MA: Harvard University Press, 2007), http://www.futureofthebook.org/gamertheory/.

12. Richard J. Light, "Writing and Student Engagement," *Peer Review* 6, no. 1 (September 2003): 28–31; Uri Treisman, "Studying Students Studying Calculus: A Look at the Lives of Minority Mathematics Students in College," *College Mathematics Journal* 23, no. 5 (November 1992): 362–72.

13. For more on online collaborations, see Rena M. Palloff and Keith Pratt, *Collaborating Online: Learning Together in Community* (San Francisco: Jossey-Bass, 2005), and John F. Lyons, *Teaching History Online* (New York: Routledge, 2009), 40–42.

14. Natasha Müller, *Halt! Grenze,* (2009), http://chnm.gmu.edu/freedomwith outwalls/news/mason-student-art-exhibit.html.

15. Chad Gaffield, "Toward the Coach in the History Classroom," *Canadian Issues* (Fall 2001): 12.

16. The website of the Preservation Association is http://www.honorfairfaxcem eteries.org/.

17. The database the students created is at http://mycemetery.org.

18. Kimberly Harney, "A Student's Unexpected Cemetery Discovery," Fairfax County Park Authority, *ResOURces* 11, no. 2 (Summer 2011): 8.

19. Lendol Calder, "Uncoverage: Toward a Signature Pedagogy for the History Survey," *Journal of American History* 92, no. 4 (March 2006), http://www.historyco operative.org/journals/jah/92.4/calder.html.

20. Grant P Wiggins, *Understanding by Design,* Merrill education/ASCD college textbook series, 2nd ed. (Upper Saddle River, NJ: Merrill/Prentice Hall, 2005), 17–21.

21. Michael Wesch, "The Machine is Us/ing Us," http://www.youtube.com/watch?v=6gmP4nk0EOE. Accessed June 8, 2011.

22. Edward Tufte, "PowerPoint Is Evil," *Wired,* September 2003, http://www.wired.com/wired/archive/11.09/ppt2.html. Accessed October 11, 2010.

23. John McClymer, *The AHA Guide to Teaching and Learning With New Media* (Washington, D.C: American Historical Association, 2005), 5.

24. Calder, "Uncoverage."

25. Tufte, "PowerPoint Is Evil."

26. Peter Norvig, "The Gettysburg PowerPoint Presentation," http://norvig .com/Gettysburg/. Accessed June 1, 2011.

27. David Voelker, "History and the Changing Landscape of Information: Blogging for Your Students," *Perspectives* (May 2007), http://www.historians.org/perspectives/issues/2007/0705/0705tec7.cfm.

28. See, for example, "Events: The History Student: Kathleen's History and Culture blog," http://kathleenmcil.wordpress.com/category/events/.

29. http://www.dancohen.org/clio-wired/. Accessed June 9, 2011.

30. "The ECAR Study of Undergraduate Students and Information Technology, 2010," EDUCAUSE, October 2010, 4.

31. "Twitter for Academia," *AcademHack,* January 23, 2008, http://academhack .outsidethetext.com/home/2008/twitter-for-academia/. Accessed June 23, 2011. See also Mark Sample, "Practical Advice for Teaching with Twitter," *ProfHacker,* August 25, 2010, http://chronicle.com/blogs/profhacker/practical-advice-for-teaching-with-twitter/26416. Accessed December 1, 2011.

32. http://edwired.org/2005/12/14/whither-wiki/.

33. http://edwired.org/2007/01/26/why-i-wont-get-hired-at-middlebury/.

34. Mark Phillipson, "Wikis in the Classroom: A Taxonomy," in *Wiki Writing: Collaborative Learning in the College Classroom*, ed. Robert E. Cummings and Matt Barton (Ann Arbor: University of Michigan Press, 2008), 19–43.

35. The relevant *Wikipedia* policies can be found at Wikipedia: Neutral Point of View, http://en.wikipedia.org/w/index.php?title=Wikipedia:Neutral_point_of_view&oldid=429761703; Wikipedia: No original research, http://en.wikipedia .org/w/index.php?title=Wikipedia:No_original_research&oldid=433709801; Wikipedia: Verifiability, http://en.wikipedia.org/w/index.php?title=Wikipedia:Verifiability&oldid=433820537; Wikipedia: Notability, http://en.wikipedia.org/w/index.php?title=Wikipedia:Notability&oldid=433454644. All accessed June 14, 2011.

36. Roy Rosenzweig, "Can History Be Open Source? *Wikipedia* and the Future of the Past," *Journal of American History* 93, no. 1 (June 2006): 117–46.

37. Rosenzweig, "Can History Be Open Source?"

38. Dan Gilbert, Helen L. Chen, and Jeremy Sabol, "Building Learning Communities With Wikis," 71; Thomas Nelson, "Writing in the Wikishop: Constructing Knowledge in the Electronic Classroom," in *Wiki Writing;* and Michael J. Jacobson, *Designs for Learning Environments of the Future* (New York: Springer, 2009), 150.

39. Nelson, "Writing in the Wikishop: Constructing Knowledge in the Electronic Classroom," 194–95.

40. http://en.wikipedia.org/w/index.php?title=Donner_Party&direction=prev &oldid=50577380.

41. http://en.wikipedia.org/w/index.php?title=Donner_Party&direction=next &oldid=50355986.

42. http://en.wikipedia.org/w/index.php?title=Donner_Party&oldid=5128 6585.

43. http://en.wikipedia.org/w/index.php?title=Donner_Party&oldid=43609 5208.

44. "Donner Party," http://en.wikipedia.org/w/index.php?title=Donner_Party& oldid=463503809. Accessed December 8, 2011.

45. http://en.wikipedia.org/wiki/David_and_Catherine_Birnie.

Chapter 5

1. Anonymous respondent to a survey by the American Historical Association, 2010, quoted in Robert Townsend, "Assimilation of New Media into History Teaching: Some Snapshots from the Edge," *Perspectives* (December 2010), http://www .historians.org/perspectives/issues/2010/1012/1012pro1.cfm. Accessed February 11, 2011.

2. A student in one of my history classes describing a mash-up video he created (see account of this student's work in the introduction).

3. Townsend, "Assimilation of New Media into History Teaching."

4. "User-Generated Content | Pew Research Center's Internet & American Life Project," http://www.pewinternet.org/Presentations/2006/UserGenerated-Content. aspx. "Generations 2010 | Pew Research Center's Internet & American Life Project," http://www.pewinternet.org/Reports/2010/Generations-2010.aspx. "Social Media and Young Adults | Pew Research Center's Internet & American Life Project," http://www.pewinternet.org/Reports/2010/Social-Media-and-Young-Adults.aspx.

5. "Social Media and Young Adults | Pew Research Center's Internet & American Life Project," http://www.pewinternet.org/Reports/2010/Social-Media-and-Young-Adults.aspx.

6. *Marie Antoinette* (Dir. Sofia Coppola, Sony Pictures, 2007); Seth Grahame-Smith, *Abraham Lincoln: Vampire Hunter* (New York: Grand Central Publishing, 2010); Jane Austen and Ben H. Winters, *Sense and Sensibility and Sea Monsters* (Philadelphia: Quirk Books, 2009).

7. Natalie Zemon Davis, *Slaves on Screen: Film and Historical Vision* (Cambridge, MA: Harvard University Press, 2002), 2–4.

8. Davis, *Slaves on Screen,* 4.

9. Stéphane Lévesque, *Thinking Historically: Educating Students for the Twenty-First Century* (Toronto: University of Toronto Press, 2008), 20–21.

10. Neil Stephenson, "Remixing History: The Cigar Box Project" (lecture, the K12 Online Conference 2010, Calgary, Alberta, 2009), http://k12onlineconference .org/?p=459.

11. "Little man vs. big machine," 2006, http://www.youtube.com/watch?v=u7M f9j8co70&feature=youtube_gdata.

12. Davis, *Slaves on Screen,* 2. See also Peter Lambert and Philip Schofield, *Making History: An Introduction to the History and Practices of a Discipline* (London: Routledge, 2004), 251–53.

13. "An Anthropological Introduction to YouTube," 2008, http://www.youtube.com/watch?v=TPAO-lZ4_hU&feature=youtube_gdata.

14. Amy Burvall and Herb Mahelona, "What I Learned from Napoleon and MTV," TEDxHonolulu, November 22, 2011: http://www.youtube.com/user/historyteachers?blend=1&ob=video-mustangbase#p/a/f/0/44jxjM_7jnY. Accessed December 27, 2011.

15. T. Mills Kelly, "Why I Won't Get Hired at Middlebury," *Edwired,* January 26, 2007, http://edwired.org/2007/01/26/why-i-wont-get-hired-at-middlebury/.

16. On how important it is to let young people be creative online, see Mizuko Ito et al., *Hanging Out, Messing Around, and Geeking Out: Kids Living and Learning with New Media* (Cambridge, MA: MIT Press, 2010), 243–93.

17. Yoni Applebaum, "How the Professor Who Fooled *Wikipedia* Got Caught By Reddit," The Atlantic.com, May 15, 2012.

18. *Edward Owens: Discussion,* http://en.wikipedia.org/wiki/Wikipedia:Articles_for_deletion/Edward_Owens. Accessed June 27, 2011. In January 2011, the Edwards Owens hoax even made TechWorld.com's list of the Top Ten hoaxes in *Wikipedia* history: http://features.techworld.com/applications/3256949/the-10-biggest-hoaxes-in-wikipedias-first-10-years/.

19. Carl Becker, "Everyman His Own Historian," December 29, 1931, http://www.historians.org/info/AHA_history/clbecker.htm.

20. Thucydides, *The Peloponnesian War,* trans. Richard Crawley (New York: E. P. Dutton & Co., 1914), 14–15.

21. Bruce A. VanSledright, "Can Ten-Year-Olds Learn to Investigate History as Historians Do?" *OAH Newsletter* (August 2000), http://www.oah.org/pubs/nl/2000aug/vansledright.html. See also Lévesque, *Thinking Historically,* 11. For a full description of what I did in that fifth grade class, see "I'll Go First": http://www.playingwithhistory.com/ill-go-first/.

22. For a more complete description of what happened with those fifth graders, see T. Mills Kelly, "I'll Go First," *Playing With Technology in History,* http://www.playingwithhistory.com/ill-go-first/. Accessed May 12, 2010.

23. On why blaming students is a bad idea, see Uri Treisman, "Studying Students Studying Calculus: A Look at the Lives of Minority Mathematics Students in College," *College Mathematics Journal* 23, no. 5 (November 1992): 362–72; Carl Wieman and Kathleen Perkins, "Transforming Physics Education," *Physics Today* 58, no. 11 (2005): 36–41.

24. John Jeremiah Sullivan, "Violence of the Lambs," *GQ,* February 2008, 118–21, 187–91.

25. The syllabus is available at http://chnm.gmu.edu/history/faculty/kelly/blogs/h389/f08syl.pdf. The class blog, which the students stopped using midsemester once they started work on their hoax, is at http://chnm.gmu.edu/history/faculty/kelly/blogs/h389/.

26. The books assigned in the course were John Mitchinson and John Lloyd,

The Book of General Ignorance; Robert Harris, *Selling Hitler: The Extraordinary Story of the Con Job of the Century;* Robert Silverberg, *Scientists and Scoundrels: A Book of Hoaxes;* and Michael Farquhar, *A Treasury of Deception: Liars, Misleaders, Hoodwinkers, and the Extraordinary True Stories of History's Greatest Hoaxes, Fakes and Frauds.* The video of *The Old Negro Space Program* can be found at http://negrospacepro gram.com/blog/nsp-movie. For more on the Czech Dream, see *Český sen,* http:// www.imdb.com/title/tt0402906/.

27. See, for instance, John Biggs, "The Junkman's Dilemma: How the Internet Has Changed How We See History," TechCrunch.com, May 6, 2012, and Brendon Fitzgerald, "Here There Be Monsters," TheMorningNews.org, September 14, 2012.

28. Finding out about the real Edward Owens taught my students how to use genealogical databases such as Ancestry.com. According to the U.S. Census of 1910, the Edward Owens who lived in the region was fifty-seven years old and so would have been twelve when the Civil War ended in 1865. If anyone interested in the project had bothered to check this fact, the entire house of cards would have collapsed, but the students assumed, correctly it turned out, that no one would go to that much trouble.

29. http://lastamericanpirate.net/2008/09/03/hello-world/index.html.

30. The videos created by the class can be seen at http://www.youtube.com/user/ janebrowning. Their version of the *Wikipedia* entry is at http://en.wikipedia.org/w/ index.php?title=Edward_Owens&oldid=256742352.

31. See the official website of International Talk Like a Pirate Day at http://www .talklikeapirate.com/.

32. See, for example, Jim Groom's blog, *bavatuesdays,* at http://bavatuesdays .com/the-last-american-pirate/.

33. http://twitter.com/digitalhumanist/status/1036654663.

34. Groom, *bavatuesdays,* http://bavatuesdays.com/the-last-american-pirate/.

35. http://lastamericanpirate.net/2008/12/03/videos/index.html#comments.

36. See, for instance, Jennifer Howard, "Teaching by Lying: Professor Unveils 'Last Pirate' Hoax," *Chronicle of Higher Education,* December 19, 2008, http:// chronicle.com/article/Teaching-by-Lying-Professor/1420, and Jerry Griffith, "Pirates," http://www.youtube.com/watch?v=6RT9ZwlNLeY. For reactions to the hoax in the blogosphere, see the following posts in my blog, *Edwired,* http://ed wired.org/?p=418, and http://edwired.org/?p=446. As a postscript to this particular controversy, had any of those taken in by the hoax bothered to look up the domain registry, they would have seen it belongs to me, not to Jane Browning: http://whois .domaintools.com/lastamericanpirate.net.

37. Thomas J. Scott and Michael K. O'Sullivan, "Analyzing Student Search Strategies: Making a Case for Integrating Information Literacy Skills into the Curriculum—Technology News—redOrbit," *Teacher Librarian* 33, no. 1 (October 2005), http:// www.redorbit.com/news/technology/290927/analyzing_student_search_strategies_ making_a_case_for_integrating_information/.

38. Lévesque, *Thinking Historically,* 27.

39. Comment by Kelly on "Was the Last American Pirate 'Authentic'?" Edwired .org, April 13, 2010.

40. H. L. Mencken, "A Neglected Anniversary," *New York Evening Mail*, December 28, 1917.

41. http://doctorbs.blogspot.com/2009/01/how-do-you-know-its-true.html.

42. Beverley C. Southgate, *History Meets Fiction,* 1st ed. (Harlow, England: Pearson/Longman, 2009), 153.

43. "BERT IS EVIL - The Only Official Evil Portal," http://www.bertisevil.tv/.

44. Roy Rosenzweig, "Scarcity or Abundance? Preserving the Past in a Digital Era," *American Historical Review* 108, no. 3 (June 2003): 735–62. The Bert website now lives at http://www.bertisevil.tv. On the disappearing Trotsky, see "The Commissar Vanishes," http://www.newseum.org/berlinwall/commissar_vanishes/index .htm. Accessed May 25, 2010.

45. http://lastamericanpirate.net/2008/11/12/last-will-and-testament-of-edward-owens/index.html.

46. Comment by Kristin M. on "You Were Warned," Edwired.org, January 3, 2009.

47. On these two controversies, see "How the Ambrose Story Developed," *History News Network,* http://hnn.us/articles/504.html; "How the Goodwin Story Developed," *History News Network,* http://hnn.us/articles/590.html. Both accessed May 25, 2010.

48. On ethics in history education, see Lendol Calder, "Not Dr. Laura," *Reviews in American History* 28, no. 2 (2000): 318–26; "How the Ambrose Story Developed," http://hnn.us/articles/504.html.

49. Southgate, *History Meets Fiction,* 23.

50. *Four Point Report,* January 4, 2009, http://fourpointreport.com/blog/?p=117. Accessed June 27, 2010. The *Four Point Report* has since been removed from the Internet.

51. *Four Point Report,* January 4, 2009, http://fourpointreport.com/blog/? p=117.

52. See, for instance, Tech Therapy, "*Wikipedia*'s Co-Founder Calls for Better Information Literacy," http://chronicle.com/article/Audio-Wikipedias-Co-Founder/65841/. In this podcast interview Jimmy Wales describes himself as "really, really, really" annoyed by projects such as those undertaken in this class. He does, however, admit to having been unfamiliar with the course until the podcast host posed a question about it.

53. http://edwired.org/?p=418#comment-28716.

54. "discovery and creation . . . and lies," info-fetishist.org, http://info-fetishist .org/2009/01/03/discovery-and-creation-and-lies/. Accessed May 26, 2010.

55. "Edward Owens, "Pirate and Hoax: Shiver Me Timbers!," Cathy Davidson (HASTAC), http://www.hastac.org/node/1858. Accessed May 26, 2010.

56. Comment by Kelly on "Was the Last American Pirate Authentic?" http:// edwired.org/?p=608#comments.

57. For a further meditation on pushing the boundaries of our understanding of the relationships between historical and geographical information, see Jo Guldi, *Inscape,* http://landscape.blogspot.com/ Accessed August 15, 2010.

58. Pyramid at Chichen Itza, http://www.thingiverse.com/thing:4155.

59. Gothic Cathedral Play Set, http://www.thingiverse.com/thing:2030.

Conclusion

1. Felix Gillette, "The Rise and Inglorious Fall of MySpace," *Business-Week,* June 22, 2011, http://www.businessweek.com/magazine/content/11_27/b4235053917570.htm.

2. "Friendster," *Wikipedia,* http://en.wikipedia.org/wiki/Friendster. Accessed June 20, 2011.

3. "Google Geo Developers Blog: Big Birthday . . . Google Maps API Turns 5!," *Google Geo Developers Blog,* June 29, 2010, http://googlegeodevelopers.blogspot.com/2010/06/big-birthday-google-maps-api-turns-5.html.

4. Weaving History, http://www.weavinghistory.org/. Accessed June 29, 2011.

Bibliography

Aditi, Muralidharan. "Text Mining 19th Century Novels with the Stanford Literature Lab." Text Mining and the Digital Humanities, May 11, 2010. http://min inghumanities.com/2010/05/11/text-mining-19th-century-novels-with-the-stanford-humanities-computing-lab/.

Aiden, Erez Lieberman, and Jean-Baptiste Michel. "What We Learned from 5 Million Books," 2011. http://www.youtube.com/watch?v=5l4cA8zSreQ&feature=y outube_gdata_player.

Allan Howard. "American Studies and the New Technologies: New Paradigms for Teaching and Learning." *Rethinking History* 8, no. 2 (June 2004): 277–91.

Allardyce, Gilbert. "The Rise and Fall of the Western Civilization Course." *American Historical Review* 87, no. 3 (June 1982): 695–725.

American Historical Association, The. *The Next Generation of History Teachers,* 2007. http://www.historians.org/pubs/free/historyteaching/index.htm.

Applebaum, Yoni. "How the Professor Who Fooled Wikipedia Got Caught By Reddit," The Atlantic.com, May 15, 2012.

Argamon, Shlomo, Jean-Baptiste Goulain, Russell Horton, and Mark Olsen. "Vive la Différence! Text Mining Gender Difference in French Literature." *DHQ: Digital Humanities Quarterly* 3, no. 2 (Spring 2009).

Arrington, Michael. "85% of College Students Use FaceBook." *TechCrunch,* September 7, 2005. http://techcrunch.com/2005/09/07/85-of-college-students-use-facebook/.

Atkins, Annette. "A Teaching Strategy: Teaching U.S. History Backwards." *Perspectives* (March 2000).

Auerbach, Jerold S. "Victory Lap." *Chronicle of Higher Education,* September 16, 2010. http://chronicle.com/article/Victory-Lap/124383/?sid=ja&utm_source=ja&utm_medium=en.

Austen, Jane. *Sense and Sensibility and Sea Monsters.* Philadelphia: Quirk Books, 2009.

Autrey, Tara M., Cathy O'Berry Edington, Troy Hicks, Aram Kabodian, Nicole Lerg, Rebecca Luft-Gardner, Anne Russo, and Rebecca Stephens. "More than Just a Web Site: Representing Teacher Research through Digital Portfolios." *English Journal* 95, no. 2 (November 2005): 65–70.

Avran, Lanny. "Teaching with Blogs." *Inside Higher Ed,* July 27, 2010. http://www.insidehighered.com/views/2010/07/27/arvan.

Axtell, James. "The Pleasures of Teaching History." *History Teacher* 34, no. 4 (August 2001).

Ayers, Edward L. "The Pasts and Futures of Digital History," 1999. http://www.vcdh.virginia.edu/PastsFutures.html.

Bain, Robert B. "Into the Breach. Using Research and Theory to Shape History Instruction." In *Knowing, Teaching and Learning History: National and International Perspectives,* 331–352. New York: New York University Press, 2000.

Ball, Cheryl E., and Ryan M. Moeller. "Converging Assumptions." http://www.bgsu.edu/cconline/convergence/web2.html.

Barker, Elton. "Hestia Project." http://www.open.ac.uk/Arts/hestia/index.html.

Barr, Robert B., and John Tagg. "From Teaching to Learning: A New Paradigm for Undergraduate Education." *Change* 27, no. 6 (December 1995): 12–25.

Bass, Randy, and Roy Rosenzweig. *Rewiring the History and Social Studies Classroom: Needs, Frameworks, Dangers, and Proposals,* http://chnm.gmu.edu/essays-on-history-new-media/essays/?essayid=26.

Bass, Randy, and Theresa Schlafly. "Participatory Learning and the New Humanities: An Interview with Cathy Davidson." *Academic Commons,* January 7, 2009. http://www.academiccommons.org/commons/essay/participatory-learning-and-new-humanities-interview-cathy-davidson.

Bauerlein, Mark. *The Dumbest Generation: How the Digital Age Stupefies Young Americans and Jeopardizes Our Future.* New York: Penguin, 2009.

Beaupre, Daniel J. "Review: Beyond the Textbook: Teaching History Using Documents and Primary Sources." *History Teacher* 30, no. 4 (August 1997): 504–5.

Becker, Carl. "Everyman His Own Historian," December 29, 1931. http://www.historians.org/info/AHA_history/clbecker.htm.

Bell, Graeme. "The Dangers of Webcrawled Datasets." *First Monday* 15, no. 2 (February 2010). http://firstmonday.org/htbin/cgiwrap/bin/ojs/index.php/fm/article/view/2739.

Bell, J. Carleton. "Editorials: The Historic Sense." *Journal of Educational Psychology* 8, no. 5 (May 1917): 317–18.

Benmayor, Rina. "Theorizing Through Digital Stories: The Art of 'Writing Back' and 'Writing For'." *Academic Commons,* January 7, 2009. http://www.academiccommons.org/commons/essay/theorizing-through-digital-stories.

Berkin, Carol. *History Handbook.* New York: Houghton Mifflin, 2006.

Beyer, Barry K. "Using Writing to Learn in History." *History Teacher* 13, no. 2 (February 1980): 167–78.

Bingham, Adrian. "'The Digitization of Newspaper Archives: Opportunities and

Challenges for Historians'." *Twentieth Century British History* 21, no. 2 (June 2010): 225–31.

Birnbaum, Michael. "A Message for Washington on Schools: Don't Mess with Texas." *Washington Post,* April 1, 2010. http://www.washingtonpost.com/wp dyn/content/article/2010/03/31/AR2010033103989.html.

Blevins, Cameron, "The Mobile Historian." *historying.* http://historying.org/2009 /05/03/the-mobile-historian/.

Bolter, J. David. *Remediation: Understanding New Media.* Cambridge, MA: MIT Press, 1999.

Bolter, J. David. *Writing Space: Computers, Hypertext, and the Remediation of Print.* 2nd ed. Mahwah, NJ: Lawrence Erlbaum Associates, 2001.

Braasch, Jason L. G., Kimberly A. Lawless, Susan R. Goldman, Flori H. Manning, Kimberly W. Gomez, and Shaunna M. MacLeod. "Evaluating Search Results: An Empirical Analysis of Middle School Students' Use of Source Attributes to Select Useful Sources." *Journal of Educational Computing Research* 41, no. 1 (2009): 63–82.

Brawley, Sean, T. Mills Kelly, and Geoff Timmons. "SoTL and National Difference: Musings from Three Historians from Three Countries." *Arts and Humanities in Higher Education* 8 no. 1 (2009): 7–24.

Brecht, Bertolt. *Brecht on Theatre: The Development of an Aesthetic.* New York: Hill & Wang, 1977.

Brook, Pete. "Hidden Gems From the Flickr Commons." *Raw File,* July 13, 2009. http://www.wired.com/rawfile/2009/07/flickr-commons/.

Burkholder, Peter, and Anne Cross. "Video Killed the Term Paper Star?" *Academic Commons,* January 7, 2009. http://www.academiccommons.org/commons/es say/video-killed-term-paper-star-two-views.

Bush, Vannevar. "As We May Think." *Atlantic Monthly,* July 1945. http://www.the atlantic.com/magazine/archive/1969/12/as-we-may-think/3881/.

Bytwerk, Randall. "Historians and Misleading Web Sites." *H-German,* April 7, 2006. http://h-net.msu.edu/cgi-bin/logbrowse.pl?trx.

C-SPAN. "Slade Gorton Speech on the Proposed National History Standards." *C-SPAN,* January 18, 1995. http://www.c-spanarchives.org/congress/?q=node/77 531&id=7079046.

Cadava, Eduardo. *Words of Light: Theses on the Photography of History.* Princeton, NJ: Princeton University Press, 1998.

Calder, Lendol. "Not Dr. Laura." *Reviews in American History* 28, no. 2 (2000): 318–26.

Calder, Lendol. "Uncoverage: Toward a Signature Pedagogy for the History Survey." *Journal of American History* 92, no. 4 (March 2006).

Calder, Lendol, William Cutler, and T. Mills Kelly. "History Lessons: Historians and the Scholarship of Teaching and Learning." In *Disciplinary Styles in the Scholarship of Teaching and Learning,* edited by Mary Huber and Sherry Moreale (Washington, D.C.: American Association for Higher Education, 2001), 45–67.

Carr, Edward H. *What is History?* New York: Alfred A. Knopf, 1962.

Carretero, Mario, and James F. Voss, eds. *Learning and Reasoning in History.* vol. 2. International Review of History Education. Routledge, 1999.

Center for History and New Media. "Essays on History and New Media." http://chnm.gmu.edu/essays-on-history-new-media/essays/?show=teach.

Center for History and New Media. "Historical Thinking Matters." http://historicalthinkingmatters.org/.

Challener, Richard D., and Maurice Lee. "History and the Social Sciences: The Problem of Communications." *American Historical Review* 61, no. 2 (January 1956): 331–38.

Chasteen, Stephanie. "Powerpoint Meets Chalk: Ubiquitous Presenter." *The Active Class,* May 27, 2010. http://theactiveclass.com/2010/05/27/powerpoint-meets-chalk-ubiquitous-presenter/.

Chen, Ching-chih, Howard D. Wactlar, James G. Wang, and Kevin Kiernan. "Digital Imagery for Significant Cultural and Historical Materials." *International Journal on Digital Libraries* 5 (2005): 275–86.

Chen, Hsin-Liang. "An Analysis of Undergraduate Students' Search Behaviors in an Information Literacy Class." *Journal of Web Librarianship* 3, no. 4 (2009): 333–47.

Choo, Chun Wei. "Information Seeking on the Web: An Integrated Model of Browsing and Searching." *First Monday* 5, no. 2 (February 2000). http://firstmonday.org/htbin/cgiwrap/bin/ojs/index.php/fm/article/view/2716/2385.

Chronicle of Higher Education. "*Wikipedia*'s Co-Founder Calls for Better Information Literacy." http://chronicle.com/article/Audio-Wikipedias-Co-Founder/65841/.

Chung, EunKyung, and JungWon Yoon. "Categorical and Specificity Differences between User-Supplied Tags and Search Query Terms for Images. An Analysis of 'Flickr' Tags and Web Image Search Queries." *Information Research: An International Electronic Journal* 14, no. 3 (2009): 2009.

Cohen, Daniel J. "10 Most Popular History Syllabi." *Dan Cohen's Digital Humanities Blog,* January 11, 2006. http://www.dancohen.org/blog/posts/10_most_popular_history_syllabi.

Cohen, Daniel J. "By the Book: Assessing the Place of Textbooks in U.S. Survey Courses." *Journal of American History* 91, no. 4 (March 2005).

Cohen, Daniel J. "Digital History: The Raw and the Cooked." *Rethinking History* 8, no. 2 (June 2004): 337–40.

Cohen, Daniel J. "Enhancing Historical Research with Text-Mining and Analysis Tools." *Dan Cohen's Digital Humanities Blog,* February 4, 2008. http://www.dancohen.org/2008/02/04/enhancing-historical-research-with-text-mining-and-analysis-tools/.

Cohen, Daniel J. "History and the Second Decade of the Web." *Rethinking History* 8, no. 2 (June 2004): 293–301.

Cohen, Daniel J. "It's About Russia." *Dan Cohen's Digital Humanities Blog,* March 6, 2007. http://www.dancohen.org/2007/03/06/its-about-russia/.

Cohen, Daniel J. "Million Books Workshop Wrap-up." *Dan Cohen's Digital Hu-*

manities Blog, May 24, 2007. http://www.dancohen.org/2007/05/24/million-books-workshop-wrap-up/.

Cohen, Daniel J. "Web of Lies? Historical Knowledge on the Internet." *First Monday* 10, no. 12 (December 2005). http://firstmonday.org/htbin/cgiwrap/bin/ojs/index.php/fm/article/view/1299.

Cohen, Daniel J., and Roy Rosenzweig. "No Computer Left Behind." *Chronicle of Higher Education,* February 24, 2006. http://chnm.gmu.edu/essays-on-history-new-media/essays/?essayid=38.

Cohen, Daniel J., and Roy Rosenzweig. *Digital History: A Guide to Gathering, Preserving, and Presenting the Past on the Web.* Philadelphia: University of Pennsylvania Press, 2005.

Cohen, Patricia. "Great Caesar's Ghost! Are Traditional History Courses Vanishing?" *New York Times,* July 10, 2009.

Cohen, Patricia. "Humanities Scholars Embrace Digital Technology." *New York Times,* November 16, 2010. http://www.nytimes.com/2010/11/17/arts/17digital.html?_r=1.

Cohen, Patricia. "Victorian Literature, Statistically Analyzed with New Process." *New York Times,* December 3, 2010. http://www.nytimes.com/2010/12/04/books/04victorian.html?_r=1&pagewanted=all.

Cole, Rob W. "Intellectual History: The Pedagogy of a 'Usable Past'." http://h05.cgpublisher.com/proposals/457/index_html.

"The Computational Turn." http://sites.google.com/site/dmberry/home.

"Content-Based Image Retrieval." *Digital Humanities and Arts,* http://www.arts-humanities.net/wiki/content_based_image_retrieval_cbir_art_history.

Coopman, Stephanie J. "A Critical Examination of Blackboard's e-Learning Environment." *First Monday* 14, no. 6 (June 2009). http://firstmonday.org/htbin/cgiwrap/bin/ojs/index.php/fm/article/view/2434.

Coppola, Sofia. *Marie Antoinette.* Sony Pictures, 2007.

Coventry, Michael, Peter Felten, David Jaffee, Cecilia O'Leary, and Tracey Weis. "Ways of Seeing: Evidence and Learning in the History Classroom." *Journal of American History* 92, no. 4 (March 2006). http://www.historycooperative.org/journals/jah/92.4/coventry.html.

Cox, Richard J. "Machines in the Archive: Technology and the Coming Transformation of Archival Reference." *First Monday* 12, no. 11 (November 2007). http://firstmonday.org/htbin/cgiwrap/bin/ojs/index.php/fm/article/view/2029.

Crampton, Jeremy W. "Will Peasants Map? Hyperlinks, Map Mashups, and the Future of Information." In *The Hyperlinked Society,* edited by Joseph Turow and Lokman Tsui, 206–26. Digital Culture. Ann Arbor: University of Michigan Press, 2008.

Crane, Gregory. "What Do You Do with a Million Books?" *D-Lib Magazine,* March 2006. http://www.dlib.org/dlib/march06/crane/03crane.html.

Cullen, Jim. *Essaying the Past: How to Read, Write, and Think About History.* Chichester, England: Wiley-Blackwell, 2009.

Cummings, Robert E., and Matt Barton, eds. *Wiki Writing: Collaborative Learning in the College Classroom*. Ann Arbor: University of Michigan Press, 2008.

Davidson, Cathy. "Mobile Humanities," *HASTAC*, May 26, 2008.

Davidson, Cathy, David Theo Goldberg, and Zoe Marie Jones. *The Future of Learning Institutions in a Digital Age*. Cambridge, MA: MIT Press, June 2009.

Davies, Ian. *Debates in History Teaching*. New York: Routledge, 2011.

Davis, Natalie Zemon. *Slaves on Screen: Film and Historical Vision*. Cambridge, MA: Harvard University Press, 2002.

Davison, Graeme. "History and Hypertext." *Electronic Journal of Australian and New Zealand History* (August 1997). http://www.jcu.edu.au/aff/history/articles/davison.htm.

Dennis, Brian, Carl Smith, and Jonathan Smith. "Using Technology, Making History: A Collaborative Experiment in Interdisciplinary Teaching and Scholarship." *Rethinking History* 8, no. 2 (June 2004): 303–17.

Deselaers, Thomas, and Vittorio Ferrari. "Global and Efficient Self-Similarity for Object Classification and Detection." San Francisco, CA, 2010. http://thomas.deselaers.de/publications/papers/deselaers-evpr10.pdf.

"Destitute Pea Pickers in California. Mother of Seven Children. Age thirty-two. Nipomo, California," http://loc.gov/pictures/resource/fsa.8b29516/.

Dewey, John. *Experience and Education*. 60th ed. West Lafayette, IN: Kappa Delta Pi, 1998.

"Digital Harlem: Everyday Life 1915–1930," http://acl.arts.usyd.edu.au/harlem/.

"Dorothea Lange's 'Migrant Mother' Photographs in the Farm Security Administration Collection." http://www.loc.gov/rr/print/list/128_migm.html.

Douglass, Jeremy. "Software Studies: Cultural Pattern Recognition, or Seeing Through Images: Automatic Analysis of Visual Media and User Interactions." *Softwarestudies.com*, November 7, 2008. http://lab.softwarestudies.com/2008/05/seeing-through-images-content-analysis.html.

Dunlap, Joni. "Using Blogs for Educational Purposes." *Thoughts on Teaching*, March 16, 2008. http://thoughtsonteaching-jdunlap.blogspot.com/2008/03/using-blogs-with-students.html.

Dunning, Alastair, Ian Gregory, and Andrew Hardie. "Freeing Up Digital Content with Text Mining: New Research Means New Licenses." *Serials: The Journal for the Serials Community* 22, no. 2 (January 2009): 166–73.

Eamon, Michael. "A 'Genuine Relationship with the Actual': New Perspectives on Primary Sources, History and the Internet in the Classroom." *History Teacher* 39, no. 3 (May 2006): 297–314.

Eisenstein, Elizabeth L. *The Printing Press as an Agent of Change: Communications and Cultural Transformations in Early-Modern Europe*. New York: Cambridge University Press, 1979.

Estes, Todd. "Constructing the Syllabus: Devising a Framework for Helping Students Learn to Think Like Historians." *History Teacher* 40, no. 2 (February 2007).

Evans, Charles T., and Robert Brown. "Teaching the History Survey Course Using Multimedia Techniques." *Perspectives* 36, no. 2 (February 1998).

Evans, Sara, and Roy Rosenzweig. "Introduction." *Journal of American History* 78, no. 4 (March 1992): 1377–79.

Farrand, Max. "Report of the Conference on History in the College Curriculum," American Historical Association, Washington, D.C., 1906.

Fast, Karl V., and D. Grant Campbell. "'I Still Like Google': University Student Perceptions of Searching OPACs and the Web." In *Proceedings of the American Society for Information Science and Technology* 41 (2004): 138–46.

Fink, L. Dee. *Creating Significant Learning Experiences: An Integrated Approach to Designing College Courses.* San Francisco: Jossey-Bass, 2003.

Fink, Leon. "New Tidings For History Education, Or Lessons We Should Have Learned By Now." *History Teacher* 34, no. 2 (February 2001): 235–42.

Fling, Fred Morrow, and Howard Walter Caldwell. *Studies in European and American History.* J. H. Miller, 1897.

Friedman, Adam. "Digital Primary Source Use: Does Training Matter?" In *Society for Information Technology & Teacher Education International Conference 2005,* edited by Caroline Crawford, Roger Carlsen, Ian Gibson, Karen McFerrin, Jerry Price, Roberta Weber, and Dee Anna Willis, 3821–28. Phoenix: AACE, 2005.

Friedman, Adam. "Using Digital Primary Sources to Teach World History and World Geography: Practices, Promises, and Provisos," May 2005. http://mcel .pacificu.edu/jahc/2005/issue1/articles/friedman.php.

Friedman, Adam, and Sara Kajder. "Perceptions of Beginning Teacher Education Students Regarding Educational Technology." In *Society for Information Technology & Teacher Education International Conference 2004,* edited by Richard Ferdig, Caroline Crawford, Roger Carlsen, Niki Davis, Jerry Price, Roberta Weber, and Dee Anna Willis, 4093–97. Atlanta: AACE, 2004.

Frye, David. "Can Students Write Their Own Textbooks? Thoughts on a New Type of Writing Assignment." *History Teacher* 32, no. 4 (August 1999): 517–23.

Gaffield, Chad. "Toward the Coach in the History Classroom." *Canadian Issues* (October 2001): 12–14.

Galgano, Michael J., J. Chris Arndt, and Raymond M. Hyser. *Doing History: Research and Writing in the Digital Age.* New York: Wadsworth Publishing, 2007.

Gao, Fei, and David Wong. "Student Engagement in Distance Learning Environments: A Comparison of Threaded Discussion Forums and Text-Focused Wikis." *First Monday* 13, no. 1 (January 2008). http://firstmonday.org/htbin/cgi wrap/bin/ojs/index.php/fm/article/view/2018.

Gardiner, Lion F., George Washington University, ERIC Clearinghouse on Higher Education, Association for the Study of Higher Education, and New Jersey Institute for Collegiate Teaching and Learning. *Redesigning Higher Education: Producing Dramatic Gains in Student Learning.* ASHE-ERIC Higher Education Report 7, 1994. Washington, D.C: Graduate School of Education and Human Development, George Washington University, 1994.

Gardiner, Lion F. "Why We Must Change: The Research Evidence." *Thought & Action* 14, no. 1 (Spring 1998): 71–88.

Gasteiner, Martin, and Peter Haber. *Digitale Arbeitstechniken: für die Geistes- und Kulturwissenschaften.* Stuttgart, UTB, 2010.

Gibson, William. "God's Little Toys." *Wired,* July 2005. http://www.wired.com/wired/archive/13.07/gibson.html.

Gillette, Felix. "The Rise and Inglorious Fall of Myspace." *BusinessWeek,* June 22, 2011. http://www.businessweek.com/magazine/content/11_27/b4235053917570.htm.

Graff, Gerald. *Clueless in Academe: How Schooling Obscures the Life of the Mind.* New Haven, CT: Yale University Press, 2003.

Grahame-Smith, Seth. *Abraham Lincoln: Vampire Hunter.* New York: Grand Central Publishing, 2010.

Green, David, and Michael Roy. "Things to Do While Waiting for the Future to Happen: Building Cyberinfrastructure for the Liberal Arts." *EDUCAUSE Review* 43, no. 4 (August 2008). http://connect.educause.edu/Library/EDUCAUSE+Review/ThingstoDoWhileWaitingfor/46969?time=1229037153.

Griffith, Maggie, and Zizi Papacharissi. "Looking for You: An Analysis of Video Blogs." *First Monday* 15, no. 1 (January 2010). http://firstmonday.org/htbin/cgiwrap/bin/ojs/index.php/fm/article/view/2769.

Griffith, Robert. "Un-Tangling the Web of Cold War Studies; or, How One Historian Stopped Worrying and Learned to Love the Internet." *Journal for MultiMedia History* 3 (2000). http://www.albany.edu/jmmh/vol3/untangling/untangling.html.

Griffiths, Jillian. "Student Searching Behavior and the Web: Use of Academic Resources and Google." *Library Trends* 53, no. 4 (Spring 2005): 539–54.

Grossman, Jim. "Historical Malpractice and the Writing of Textbooks." *Perspectives* (December 2010).

Gwizdka, Jacek. "What a Difference a Tag Cloud Makes: Effects of Tasks and Cognitive Abilities on Search Results Interface Use." *Information Research: An International Electronic Journal* 14, no. 4 (December 2009). http://www.eric.ed.gov/ERICWebPortal/contentdelivery/servlet/ERICServlet?accno=EJ869366.

Hart Research Associates. *Raising The Bar: Employers' Views On College Learning In The Wake Of The Economic Downturn.* Washington, D.C., January 2010.

Haskins, Charles H. "Report of the Conference on the First Year of College Work in History." American Historical Association, Washington, D.C., 1906.

Head, Alison J. "Beyond Google: How Do Students Conduct Academic Research?" *First Monday* 12, no. 8 (August 2007). http://firstmonday.org/htbin/cgiwrap/bin/ojs/index.php/fm/article/view/1998.

Head, Alison J., and Michael B. Eisenberg. "How Today's College Students use *Wikipedia* for Course-Related Research." *First Monday* 15, no. 3 (March 2010). http://www.uic.edu/htbin/cgiwrap/bin/ojs/index.php/fm/article/view/2830/2476.

Heer, Jeffrey, Michael Bostock, and Vadim Ogievetsky. "A Tour through the Visualization Zoo—ACM Queue." *ACMQueue*, May 13, 2010. http://queue.acm.org/detail.cfm?id=1805128.

Heroes, "The Tank Man," 2008. http://www.youtube.com/watch?v=mrQqDqOx3KY&feature=youtube_gdata.

Hinsdale, Burke Aaron. *How to Study and Teach History.* New York: D. Appleton and Company, 1897.

"The History Student." *The History Student: Kathleen's History and Culture Blog.* http://kathleenmcil.wordpress.com/category/events/.

Holmberg, Kim, and Isto Huvila. "Learning Together Apart: Distance Education in a Virtual World." *First Monday* 13, no. 10 (October 2008). http://firstmonday.org/htbin/cgiwrap/bin/ojs/index.php/fm/article/view/2178.

Horton, Sarah. *Web Teaching Guide.* New Haven, CT: Yale University Press, 2000.

Huberman, Bernardo, Daniel M. Romero, and Fang Wu. "Social Networks That Matter: Twitter under the Microscope." *First Monday* 14, no. 1 (January 2009). http://firstmonday.org/htbin/cgiwrap/bin/ojs/index.php/fm/article/view/2317.

"Hypercities," University of California, Los Angeles. http://hypercities.com/.

Iggers, Georg G., and James M. Powell, eds. *Leopold Von Ranke and the Shaping of the Historical Discipline.* Syracuse, NY: Syracuse University Press, 1990.

Ignacio, Dino. "BERT IS EVIL—The Only Official Evil Portal." http://funkatron.com/bert/bert.htm.

Institute of Historical Research. "Connected Histories: Sources for Building British History, 1500–1900." *IHR Digital,* March 31, 2011. http://www.history.ac.uk/connectedhistories.

Ito, Mizuko, Becky Herr-Stephenson, Dan Perkel, and Christo Sims. *Hanging Out, Messing Around, and Geeking Out.* Cambridge, MA: MIT Press, 2009.

Jacobson, Michael J. *Designs for Learning Environments of the Future.* New York: Springer, 2009.

Jaffee, David. "'Scholars Will Soon Be Instructed Through the Eye': E-Supplements and the Teaching of U.S. History." *Journal of American History* 89, no. 4 (March 2003).

John Nicholas Brown Center. "Mobile Social History Digital Humanities Project," August 10, 2009. http://proteus.brown.edu/jnbc/817.

Jones, Steve, Camille Johnson-Yale, Sarah Millermaier, and Francisco Seoane Perez. "Everyday Life, Online: U.S. College Students' Use of the Internet." *First Monday* 14, no. 10 (October 2009). http://firstmonday.org/htbin/cgiwrap/bin/ojs/index.php/fm/article/view/2649.

Keller, Clair W. "Adding Inquiry to the 'Inquiry' Method." *History Teacher* 4, no. 1 (1970): 47–53.

Kelly, Henry. "Continuous Improvement in Undergraduate Education: A Possible Dream." *Innovations: Technology, Governance, Globalization* 3, no. 3 (July 2008): 133–51.

Kelly, Kevin. "Scan This Book!" *New York Times,* May 14, 2006. http://www.nytimes.com/2006/05/14/magazine/14publishing.html?pagewanted=4.

Kelly, T. Mills. "Before Plugging In, Consider Your Options." *Chronicle Review,* July 13, 2001.

Kelly, T. Mills. "But Mine's Better: Teaching Students in the Digital Age." *History Teacher* 44 no. 3 (May 2011): 369–78.

Kelly, T. Mills. "For Better or Worse? The Marriage of the Web and Classroom." *Journal of the Association for History and Computing* 3, no. 2 (August 2000). http://mcel.pacificu.edu/jahc/2000/issue2/articles/kelly/.

Kelly, T. Mills. "Remaking Liberal Education. The Challenges of New Media." *Academe* (January–February 2003): 28–31.

Kelly, T. Mills. "The Role of Technology in World History Teaching." *World History Connected* 3, no. 3 (July 2006). http://worldhistoryconnected.press.illinois.edu/3.3/kelly.html.

Kelly, T. Mills. "Toward Transparency in Teaching: Publishing a Course Portfolio." *Perspectives* (November 2001): 26–28.

Kelly, T. Mills. "Using New Media to Teach East European History." *Nationalities Papers* 29, no. 3 (2001): 499–507.

Kelly, T. Mills. "Why I Won't Get Hired at Middlebury." *Edwired,* January 26, 2007. http://edwired.org/2007/01/26/why-i-wont-get-hired-at-middlebury/.

Kevin, Drum. "The Mirror of History." *Washington Monthly,* April 27, 2003. http://www2.washingtonmonthly.com/archives/individual/2003_04/001046.php.

Kim, Jeff, Elan Lee, Timothy Thomas, and Caroline Dombrowski. "Storytelling in New Media: The Case of Alternate Reality Games, 2001–2009." *First Monday* 14, no. 6 (June 2009). http://firstmonday.org/htbin/cgiwrap/bin/ojs/index.php/fm/article/view/2484.

Kim, Kyung-Sun, and Joi Moore. "Web-Based Learning: Factors Affecting Students' Satisfaction and Learning Experience." *First Monday* 10, no. 11 (November 2005). http://firstmonday.org/htbin/cgiwrap/bin/ojs/index.php/fm/article/view/1294.

Kornblith, Gary J., and Carol Lasser. "Beyond Best Practices: Taking Seriously the Scholarship of Teaching and Learning." *Journal of American History* 92, no. 4 (March 2006).

Kornblith, Gary J., and Carol Lasser. "More than Bells and Whistles? Using Digital Technology to Teach American History." *Journal of American History* 89, no. 4 (March 2003).

Kornblith, Gary J., and Carol Lasser. "Teaching the American History Survey at the Opening of the Twenty-First Century: A Round Table Discussion." *Journal of American History* 87, no. 4 (2001).

Kuhn, Thomas S. *The Structure of Scientific Revolutions.* 3rd ed. Chicago: University of Chicago Press, 1996.

Kulish, Nicholas. "Author, 17, Says It's 'Mixing,' Not Plagiarism." *New York Times,* February 12, 2010. http://www.nytimes.com/2010/02/12/world/europe/12germany.html.

Lagoze, Carl, Dean B. Kraft, Sandy Payette, and Susan Jesuroga. "What Is a Digital Library Anyway?" *D-Lib Magazine,* November 2005. http://www.dlib.org/dlib/november05/lagoze/11lagoze.html.

Lambert, Peter, and Philip Schofield, eds. *Making History: An Introduction to the History and Practices of a Discipline*. London: Routledge, 2004.

Landow, George P. *Hypertext 2.0*. Baltimore: Johns Hopkins University Press, 1997.

Lane, Lisa. "Insidious Pedagogy: How Course Management Systems Affect Teaching." *First Monday* 14, no. 10 (October 2009). http://firstmonday.org/htbin/cgi wrap/bin/ojs/index.php/fm/article/view/2530.

Lavoie, Brian, Lynn Silipigni Connaway, and Lorcan Dempsey. "Anatomy of Aggregate Collections." *D-Lib Magazine*, September 2005. http://www.dlib.org/dlib/september05/lavoie/09lavoie.html.

Lee, John. "Pre-service Social Studies Teachers' Reckoning with Historical Interpretations and Controversy Arising from the Use of Digital Historical Resources." *Journal of the Association for History and Computing* 4, no. 2 (August 2001). http://www.mcel.pacificu.edu/jahc/2001/issue2/reports/lee/.

Lehner, Kristin, Kelly Schrum, and T. Mills Kelly. *World History Matters: A Student Guide to World History Online*. Bedford/St. Martin's, 2008.

Lenhart, Amanda. *User-Generated Content*. Pew Internet & American Life Project, November 6, 2006. http://www.pewinternet.org/Presentations/2006/UserGenerated-Content.aspx.

Lenhart, Amanda, Kristen Purcell, Aaron Smith, and Kathryn Zickuhr. *Social Media and Young Adults*. Pew Research Center's Internet & American Life Project, February 3, 2010. http://www.pewinternet.org/Reports/2010/Social-Media-and-Young-Adults.aspx.

Lévesque, Stephane. "Discovering the Past: Engaging Canadian Students in Digital History." *Canadian Social Studies* 40, no. 1 (Summer 2006).

Lévesque, Stephane. "Journey Into the World of the School: High School Students' Understanding of Citizenship in B.C. and Quebec." PhD diss., University of British Columbia, 2001.

Lévesque, Stephane. *Thinking Historically: Educating Students for the Twenty-First Century*. Toronto: University of Toronto Press, 2008.

Lewis, Michael. "Reflections: 'This Class Will Write a Book': An Experiment in Environmental History Pedagogy." *Environmental History* 9, no. 4 (October 2004).

Li, Sophia. "Online Course Construction Gets a 'Do-It-Yourself' Web Site." *Chronicle of Higher Education: Wired Campus*, July 23, 2010.

Library of Congress. "Using Primary Sources." *Teachers*. http://www.loc.gov/teach ers/usingprimarysources/.

Light, Richard J. "Writing and Student Engagement." *Peer Review* 6, no. 1 (September 2003): 28–31.

"Light and Shadows: Emma Goldman 1910–1916." http://gray.ischool.berkeley.edu/emma/.

"Little Man vs Big Machine," 2006. http://www.youtube.com/watch?v=u7Mf9j8co 70&feature=youtube_gdata.

Lowenthal, David. "Dilemmas and Delights of Learning History." In *Knowing,*

Teaching and Learning History: National and International Perspectives, 63–82. New York: New York University Press, 2000.

Luker, Ralph E. "Were There Blog Enough and Time." *Perspectives,* May 2005.

Lyons, John F. "Teaching U.S. History Online: Problems and Prospects." *History Teacher* 37, no. 4 (August 2004): 447–56.

"Making History and Civics a Priority." *Washington Post,* June 17, 2011. http://www .washingtonpost.com/opinions/making-history-and-civics-a-priority/2011/ 06/17/AGbItYZH_story.html.

Manovich, Lev. "Cultural Pattern Recognition, or Seeing Through Images: Automatic Analysis of Visual Media and User Interactions." *software studies initiative,* November 7, 2008. http://lab.softwarestudies.com/2008/05/seeing-through-images-content-analysis.html.

Marius, Richard A., and Mel Page. *A Short Guide to Writing about History.* 7th ed. Harlow, England: Longman, 2009.

Maroney, James C., and William J. McNeill. "Teaching College History: A Critique and Historiographical Analysis," 1977.

Masur, Louis P. "'Pictures Have Now Become a Necessity': The Use of Images in American History Textbooks." *Journal of American History* 84, no. 4 (March 1998): 1409–24.

Mattiuzzo, Gino. "A Digital Renaissance: Partnering with the Italian Ministry of Cultural Heritage." *The Official Google Blog,* March 10, 2010. http://googleblog .blogspot.com/2010/03/digital-renaissance-partnering-with.html.

Maxwell, Alexander. "Ban the Bullet-Point! Content-Based PowerPoint for Historians." *History Teacher* 41, no. 1 (November 2007).

McCarthy, Todd. "Marie Antoinette." *Variety,* May 24, 2006. http://www.variety .com/review/VE1117930629.html?categoryid=31&cs=1&p=0.

McClymer, John. *The AHA Guide to Teaching and Learning With New Media.* Washington, D.C: American Historical Association, 2005.

McGlinn, Meghan. "CITE Journal—Social Studies," 2007. http://www.citejournal .org/vol7/iss1/socialstudies/article1.cfm.

McGlinn, Meghan. "Digital Narratives: Classroom: DocSouth," 2004. http://doc south.unc.edu/classroom/narratives/narratives.html.

McGonigal, Jane. "Gaming Can Make a Better World." TED.com, February 2010. http://www.ted.com/talks/jane_mcgonigal_gaming_can_make_a _better_world.html.

McKinley, Albert F. "Review: Teaching History in Elementary and Secondary Schools." *American Historical Review* 21, no. 2 (January 1916): 333–35.

McLaughlin, Andrew Cunningham, George Levi Fox, Herbert Baxter Adams, Albert Bushnell Hart, Charles Homer Haskins, Lucy Maynard Salmon, and Henry Morse Stephens. *The Study of History in Schools.* New York: Macmillan, 1899.

Morris, Errol. "Which Came First, the Chicken or the Egg? (Part One)." *Opinionator,* September 25, 2007. http://opinionator.blogs.nytimes.com/2007/09/25/ which-came-first-the-chicken-or-the-egg-part-one/.

Mosborg, Susan. "Speaking of History: How Adolescents Use Their Knowledge of History in Reading the Daily News." *Cognition and Instruction* 20, no. 3 (2002): 323–58.

Munslow, Alun. *Experiments in Rethinking History.* New York: Routledge, 2004.

Munson, Matt. "Mining and Mapping Apocalyptic Texts, Part 1." *Scholars' Lab. Works in Progress,* March 11, 2009. http://www.scholarslab.org/digital-humanities/how-digital-humanities-can-improve-my-dissertation-part-1/.

Murray, Rebecca. "Writer/Director Sofia Coppola Talks About 'Marie Antoinette'." About.com: Hollywood Movies, 2006. http://movies.about.com/od/marieantoinette/a/mariesc101006_2.htm.

Nash, Gary B. *History on Trial: Culture Wars and the Teaching of the Past.* 1st ed. New York: Alfred A. Knopf, 1997.

Natter, Tobias G., and Max Hollein, *The Naked Truth: Klimt, Schiele, Kokoschka and Other Scandals.* München: Prestel, 2005.

Nelson, Robert K., Scott Nesbit, and Andrew Torget. "The History Engine: Doing History with Digital Tools." *Academic Commons,* September 9, 2009.

New Media Consortium. *Horizon Reports.* Horizon Reports, 2011. http://www.nmc.org/publications.

Nora, Pierre, and Lawrence D. Kritzman. *Realms of Memory: Conflicts and Divisions.* New York: Columbia University Press, 1996.

Novick, Peter. *That Noble Dream: The "Objectivity Question" and the American Historical Profession.* Cambridge: Cambridge University Press, 1988.

"NS-Crimes in Vienna." http://www.ns-verbrechen.at/.

Oates, George. "Many Hands Make Light Work." *Flickr Blog,* January 16, 2008. http://blog.flickr.net/en/2008/01/16/many-hands-make-light-work/.

Oder, Norman. "Google Book Search by the Numbers." *Library Journal,* February 12, 2010. http://www.libraryjournal.com/article/CA6718929.html.

"Old Bailey Online—The Proceedings of the Old Bailey, 1674–1913—Central Criminal Court." http://www.oldbaileyonline.org/index.jsp.

Olwell, Russell. "Taking History Personally: How Blogs Connect Students Outside the Classroom." *Perspectives* (January 2008).

Ophir, Shai. "A New Type of Historical Knowledge." *Information Society: An International Journal* 26, no. 2 (2010): 144.

O'Reilly, Tim. "What Is Web 2.0." *O'Reilly Media,* http://oreilly.com/web2/archive/what-is-web-20.html.

O'Reilly, Tim, and John Battelle. "Web Squared: Web 2.0 Five Years On." Lecture presented at the Web 2.0 Summit, San Francisco, October 2009. http://www.web2summit.com/web2009/public/schedule/detail/10194.

Orrill, Robert, and Linn Shapiro. "From Bold Beginnings to an Uncertain Future: The Discipline of History and History Education." *American Historical Review* 110, no. 3 (June 2005).

Pace, David. "The Amateur in the Operating Room: History and the Scholarship of Teaching and Learning." *American Historical Review* 109, no. 4 (October 2004).

Parry, David. "Twitter for Academia." *AcademHack,* January 23, 2008. http:// academhack.outsidethetext.com/home/2008/twitter-for-academia/.

Pegg, Mike. "Big Birthday . . . Google Maps API Turns 5!" *Google Geo Developers Blog,* June 29, 2010. http://googlegeodevelopers.blogspot.com/2010/06/big-birthday-google-maps-api-turns-5.html.

Pomerantz, Linda. "Bridging the Digital Divide: Reflections on 'Teaching and Learning in the Digital Age'." *History Teacher* 34, no. 4 (August 2001): 509–22.

Pritchard, Jessica. "Picturing U.S. History: An Interactive Resource for Teaching with Visual Evidence." *AHA Today,* November 4, 2008. http://blog.historians .org/resources/645/picturing-us-history-an-interactive-resource-for-teaching-with-visual-evidence.

Rael, Patrick. "What Happened and Why? Helping Students Read and Write Like Historians." *History Teacher* 39, no. 1 (November 2005): 23–32.

Raetzer, E. Y. "The Laboratory Method in the Trenton Senior High School." *Historical Outlook* 19, no. 5 (May 1928): 215–20.

Ramsay, Stephen. "The Hermeneutics of Screwing Around; or What You Do with a Million Books." Lecture, presented at the Playing With Technology in History, Niagara-on-the-Lake, Ontario, April 2010. http://www.playingwithhistory.com.

Raymond, Matt. "How Tweet It Is!: Library Acquires Entire Twitter Archive." *Library of Congress Blog,* April 14, 2010. http://blogs.loc.gov/loc/2010/04/how-tweet-it-is-library-acquires-entire-twitter-archive/.

Reichard, David A. "How Do Students Understand the History of the American West?: An Argument for the Scholarship of Teaching and Learning." *Western Historical Quarterly* 37, no. 2 (Summer 2006).

Reinhartz, Dennis, and Stephen E. Maizlish. *Essays on Walter Prescott Webb and the Teaching of History.* 1st ed. College Station: Texas A&M University Press, 1985.

Rhem, James. "Problem-Based Learning: An Introduction." *National Teaching and Learning Forum* 8, no. 1 (December 1998). http://www.ntlf.com/html/pi/9812/ pbl_1.htm.

Rieger, Olga. "Search Engine Use Behavior of Students and Faculty: User Perceptions and Implications for Future Research." *First Monday* 14, no. 12 (December 2009). http://firstmonday.org/htbin/cgiwrap/bin/ojs/index.php/fm/article/ view/2716/2385.

Robertson, Stephen. "What's Wrong with Online Readings? Text, Hypertext, and the History Web." *History Teacher* 39, no. 4 (August 2006): 441–54.

Rosenstone, Robert A. *History on Film/Film on History.* 1st ed. Harlow, England: Longman/Pearson, 2006.

Rosenstone, Robert A. *Revisioning History: Film and the Construction of a New Past.* Princeton, NJ: Princeton University Press, 1995.

Rosenstone, Robert A. *Visions of the Past: The Challenge of Film to Our Idea of History.* Cambridge, MA: Harvard University Press, 1995.

Rosenzweig, Roy. "Can History Be Open Source? *Wikipedia* and the Future of the Past." *Journal of American History* 93, no. 1 (June 2006): 117–46.

Rosenzweig, Roy. *Clio Wired: The Future of the Past in the Digital Age.* New York: Columbia University Press, 2011.

Rosenzweig, Roy. "Digital Archives Are a Gift of Wisdom to Be Used Wisely." *Chronicle of Higher Education*, June 24, 2005, B20.

Rosenzweig, Roy. "Scarcity or Abundance? Preserving the Past in a Digital Era." *American Historical Review* 108, no. 3 (June 2003): 735–62.

Rosenzweig, Roy, and David Thelen. *The Presence of the Past.* New York: Columbia University Press, 2000.

Sanchez, Joe. "Teaching with Blogs." *EDUCAUSE*, October 2, 2008. http://www.educause.edu/blog/joesanchez/TeachingwithBlogs/166276.

Sanford, Albert H. "Review: Teaching History in Elementary and Secondary Schools (Johnson)." *School Review* 24, no. 2 (February 1916): 172–73.

Scheinfeldt, Tom. "Where's the Beef? Does Digital Humanities Have to Answer Questions?" *Found History*, May 12, 2010. http://www.foundhistory.org/2010/05/12/wheres-the-beef-does-digital-humanities-have-to-answer-questions/.

Schmied, Chad, Lori A. Berry, and Josef Chad Schrock. "The Role of Emotion in Teaching and Learning History: A Scholarship of Teaching Exploration." *History Teacher* 41, no. 4 (August 2008). http://www.historycooperative.org.mutex.gmu.edu/journals/ht/41.4/berry.html.

Scott, A. O. "Marie Antoinette—A Lonely Petit Four of a Queen." *New York Times,* October 13, 2006.

Scott, Thomas J., and Michael K. O'Sullivan. "Analyzing Student Search Strategies: Making a Case for Integrating Information Literacy Skills into the Curriculum." *Teacher Librarian* 33, no. 1 (October 2005): 21.

"Secrets of Great History Teachers." *History Matters.* Center for History and New Media. http://historymatters.gmu.edu/browse/secrets/.

Seed, Patricia. "Teaching with the Web: Two Approaches." *Perspectives* 36, no. 2 (February 1998).

Seixas, Peter. "Schweigen! die Kinder!" In *Knowing, Teaching and Learning History: National and International Perspectives,* 19–37. New York: New York University Press, 2000.

Seixas, Peter. *Theorizing Historical Consciousness.* Toronto: University of Toronto Press, 2004.

Sheffer, Edith. "Creating Lives in the Classroom." *Chronicle of Higher Education,* November 22, 2009. http://chronicle.com/article/Teaching-Matters-Creating/49211/?sid=wc&utm_source=wc&utm_medium=en.

Shopes, Linda. "Making Sense of Oral History." http://historymatters.gmu.edu/mse/oral/.

Sklar, Kathryn Kish. "Teaching Students to Become Producers of New Historical Knowledge on the Web." *Journal of American History* 88, no. 4 (March 2002).

Smith, Randall E. "History of Social Studies Education (Lit Review)." http://www.siue.edu/~resmith/chapter2.htm.

Southgate, Beverley C. *History Meets Fiction*. 1st ed. Harlow, England: Pearson/Longman, 2009.

Spradlin, Simon. "Studies in the History of History Teaching." PhD diss., University of Oklahoma, 1936.

Springer, Michelle, Beth Dulabahn, Phil Michel, Barbara Natanson, David Reser, David Woodward, and Helena Zinkham. *For the Common Good: The Library of Congress Flickr Pilot Project*. Washington, D.C: Library of Congress, October 30, 2008.

Staley, David J. *Computers, Visualization, and History: How New Technology Will Transform Our Understanding of the Past*. New York: M. E. Sharpe, 2002.

Staley, David J. "Sequential Art and Historical Narrative: A Visual History of Germany." *Journal of the Association for History and Computing* 5, no. 2 (September 2002). http://quod.lib.umich.edu/j/jahc/3310410.0005.203?rgn=main;view=fulltext.

Stephens, Robert, and Josh Thumma. "Faculty-Undergraduate Collaboration in Digital History at a Public Research University." *History Teacher* 38, no. 4 (August 2005): 525–42.

Stephenson, Neil. "Remixing History: The Cigar Box Project." Calgary, Alberta, 2009. http://k12onlineconference.org/?p=459.

Stutzman, Fred. *Student Life on the Facebook*. Chapel Hill, NC, January 8, 2006. http://fredstutzman.com/pubs/stutzman_wp3.pdf.

Su, Mila C. "Inside the Web: A Look at Digital Libraries and the Invisible/Deep Web." *Journal of Educational Technology Systems* 37, no. 1 (2009): 71–82.

Tally, Bill, and Lauren B. Goldenberg. "Fostering Historical Thinking with Digitized Primary Sources." *Journal of Research on Technology in Education* 38, no. 1 (2005): 1–21.

Tanaka, Stefan. "Intersections: History and New Media: Digital Media in History: Remediating Data and Narratives." *Perspectives* (May 2009).

"TANK MAN TANGO: How to Dance It," 2009. http://www.youtube.com/watch?v=LLFmetopbvw&feature=youtube_gdata.

Tate, Marsha Ann. "Looking for Laura Secord on the Web: Using a Famous Figure from the War of 1812 as a Model for Evaluating Historical Web Sites." *History Teacher* 38, no. 2 (February 2005): 225–40.

Taylor, Paul, and Scott Keeter. *Millennials: Confident. Connected. Open to Change.—Pew Social & Demographic Trends*. Pew Research Center, February 2010. http://pewsocialtrends.org/pubs/751/millennials-confident-connected-open-to-change.

Thompson, Bob. "Lessons We May Be Doomed To Repeat; American Historians Talk About War, But Is Anyone Listening?" *Washington Post*, January 11, 2004.

Tischler, Barbara. "Teaching World History: Issues and Possibilities." *Perspectives* (October 2009).

Tobin, Kathleen A. "To Think On Paper: Using Writing Assignments in the World History Survey." *History Teacher* 34, no. 4 (August 2001): 497–508.

Tomlinson, Roger F., *Thinking about GIS: Geographic Information System Planning for Managers*. Esri, 2003.

Townsend, Robert. "Assimilation of New Media into History Teaching: Some Snapshots from the Edge." *Perspectives* (December 2010).

Townsend, Robert. "How Is New Media Reshaping the Work of Historians?" *Perspectives* (November 2010).

Townsend, Robert. "Making History: Scholarship and Professionalization in the Discipline, 1880–1940." PhD diss., George Mason University, 2009.

Treisman, Uri. "Studying Students Studying Calculus: A Look at the Lives of Minority Mathematics Students in College." *College Mathematics Journal* 23, no. 5 (November 1992): 362–72.

Tryon, Rolla Milton. *The Teaching of History in Junior and Senior High Schools*. Boston: Ginn and Company, 1921.

Tu, Yi-Wen, Meilun Shih, and Chin-Chung Tsai. "Eighth Graders' Web Searching Strategies and Outcomes: The Role of Task Types, Web Experiences and Epistemological Beliefs." *Computers & Education* 51, no. 3 (November 2008): 1142–53.

Tufte, Edward. "PowerPoint Is Evil." *Wired,* September 2003. http://www.wired.com/wired/archive/11.09/ppt2.html.

Tufte, Edward. *The Cognitive Style of PowerPoint*. Cheshire, CT: Graphics Press, 2003.

Turkel, William. "Clustering with Compression." *Digital History Hacks (2005–08)*, June 27, 2007. http://digitalhistoryhacks.blogspot.com/2007/06/clustering-with-compression.html.

Turkel, William. "Seeing There." *Digital History Hacks (2005–08)*, June 18, 2007. http://digitalhistoryhacks.blogspot.com/2007/06/seeing-there.html.

Turkel, William. "Text Mining the DCB, Part 1." *Digital History Hacks (2005–08)*, January 28, 2006. http://digitalhistoryhacks.blogspot.com/2006/01/text-mining-dcb-part-1.html.

Turkel, William. "Text Mining the DCB, Part 6." *Digital History Hacks (2005–08)*, March 5, 2006. http://digitalhistoryhacks.blogspot.com/2006/03/text-mining-dcb-part-6.html.

Turow, Joseph, and Lokman Tsui. *The Hyperlinked Society: Questioning Connections in the Digital Age*. Ann Arbor: University of Michigan Press, 2008.

Universal Newsreels. "21 Nazi Chiefs Guilty, Nuremberg Trials 1946/10/8," 2006. http://www.youtube.com/watch?v=xcudlm6tPa0&feature=youtube_gdata.

Unsworth, John. "How Not To Read A Million Books." October 2008. http://www3.isrl.illinois.edu/~unsworth/hownot2read.html.

Unsworth, John. "New Methods for Humanities Research." Lecture, presented at the Lyman Award Lecture, National Humanities Center. November 11, 2005. http://www3.isrl.illinois.edu/~unsworth/lyman.htm.

VanSledright, Bruce A. "Can Ten-Year-Olds Learn to Investigate History As Historians Do?" *Organization of American History,* August 2000. http://www.oah.org/pubs/nl/2000aug/vansledright.html.

Vess, Deborah. "History in the Digital Age: A Study of the Impact of Interactive Resources on Student Learning." *History Teacher* 37, no. 3 (May 2004): 385–99.

Vess, Deborah. "History to Go: Why iTeach with iPods." *History Teacher* 39, no. 4 (August 2006): 479–92.

de Vise, Daniel. "Wide Web of Diversions Gets Laptops Evicted from Lecture Halls." *Washington Post,* March 9, 2010. http://www.washingtonpost.com/wpdyn/content/article/2010/03/08/AR2010030804915.html?hpid=topnews.

Voelker, David. "History and the Changing Landscape of Information: Blogging for Your Students." *Perspectives* (May 2007).

Ward, Paul. *Elements of Historical Thinking.* Washington, D.C: American Historical Association, 1971.

Wark, McKenzie. *Gamer Theory.* Cambridge, MA: Harvard University Press, 2007. http://www.futureofthebook.org/gamertheory/.

Weingartner, James J. "Trophies of War: U.S. Troops and the Mutilation of Japanese War Dead, 1941–1945." *Pacific Historical Review* 61, no. 1 (February 1992): 53–67.

Weinstein, Barbara. "The Case of the Incredible Shrinking Historians?" *Perspectives* (September 2007). http://historians.org/Perspectives/issues/2007/0709/0709pre1.cfm.

Wesch, Micheal. "A Vision of Students Today," 2007. http://www.youtube.com/watch?v=dGCJ46vyR9o&feature=youtube_gdata.

Wesch, Micheal. "An Anthropological Introduction to YouTube," 2008. http://www.youtube.com/watch?v=TPAO-lZ4_hU&feature=youtube_gdata.

Wesch, Micheal. "From Knowledgable to Knowledge-able: Learning in New Media Environments." *Academic Commons,* January 7, 2009. http://www.academiccommons.org/commons/essay/knowledgable-knowledge-able.

Wesch, Micheal. "Information R/evolution, 2007." http://www.youtube.com/watch?v=-4CV05HyAbM&feature=youtube_gdata.

Wesch, Micheal. "Web 2.0 . . . The Machine is Us/ing Us," 2007. http://www.youtube.com/watch?v=6gmP4nk0EOE&feature=youtube_gdata.

West, James A., and Margaret L. West. *Using Wikis for Online Collaboration: The Power of the Read-Write Web.* New York: Wiley, 2009.

Wichowski, Alexis. "Survival of the Fittest Tag: Folksonomies, Findability, and the Evolution of Information Organization." *First Monday* 14, no. 5 (May 2009). http://firstmonday.org/htbin/cgiwrap/bin/ojs/index.php/fm/article/view/2447.

Wieman, Carl, and Kathleen Perkins. "Transforming Physics Education." *Physics Today* 58, no. 11 (2005): 36–41.

Wiggins, Grant P., and Jay McTighe. *Understanding by Design.* New York: Pearson, 2005.

Wineburg, Daisy Martin Sam. "Seeing Thinking on the Web." *History Teacher* 41, no. 3 (May 2008).

Wineburg, Sam. "Crazy for History." *Journal of American History* 90, no. 4 (March 2004): 1401–14.

Wineburg, Sam. *Historical Thinking and Other Unnatural Acts: Charting the Future of Teaching the Past.* Philadelphia: Temple University Press, 2001.

Wineburg, Sam. "Probing the Depths of Students' Historical Knowledge." *Perspectives* (March 1992).

Wineburg, Sam, Susan Mosborg, Dan Porat, and Ariel Duncan. "Forrest Gump and the Future of Teaching the Past." *Phi Delta Kappan* 89, no. 3 (November 2007): 168–77.

Yau, Nathan. "Explorations of Real-World Traffic." *Flowing Data,* June 2, 2010. http://flowingdata.com/2010/04/15/explorations-of-real-world-traffic/.

Young, Jeff. "YouTube Better at Funny Cat Videos Than Educational Content, Professors Say." *Chronicle of Higher Education. Wired Campus,* July 26, 2010. http://chronicle.com/blogPost/YouTube-Better-at-Funny-Cat/25768/?sid=wc&utm_source=wc&utm_medium=en.

Young, Jeffrey R. "Change or Die: Scholarly E-Mail Lists, Once Vibrant, Fight for Relevance." *Chronicle of Higher Education,* June 25, 2009. http://chronicle.com/free/v55/i40/40college2.0.htm.

Young, Jeffrey R. "How Social Networking Helps Teaching (and Worries Some Professors)."*Chronicle of Higher Education,* July 22, 2010. http://chronicle.com/article/How-Social-Networking-Helps/123654/?sid=wc&utm_source=wc&utm_medium=en.

Young, William E. "Methods of Teaching and Learning." *Social Studies* 11, no. 4, part 2 (October 1941): 446–58.

Yu, Bei, Stefan Kaufmann, and Daniel Diermeier. "Classifying Party Political Affiliation from Political Speech." *Journal of Information Technology & Politics* 5, no. 1 (2008): 33–49.

Zacharek, Stephanie. "Marie Antoinette." *Salon.com,* October 13, 2006. http://www.salon.com/entertainment/movies/review/2006/10/13/marie_antoinette/index.html?CP=IMD&DN=110.

Zeiler, Michael. *Modeling Our World: The Esri Guide to Geodatabase Design.* Redlands, CA: Esri Press, 1999.

Zhang, Yin, David Robins, Jason Holmes, and Athena Salaba. "Understanding Internet Searching Performance in a Heterogeneous Portal for K–12 Students: Search Success, Search Time, Strategy, and Effort." *Journal of Web Librarianship* 3, no. 1 (January 2009): 15–33.

Zickuhr, Kathryn. *Generations 2010.* Pew Internet & American Life Project, December 16, 2010. http://www.pewinternet.org/Reports/2010/Generations-2010.aspx.